SCOTTISH STEAMERS IN THE 1930s

Compiled by Derek Crawford, Iain Quinn & Gordon Wilson
from the J B MacGeorge Collection

This book is dedicated to the masters and crew of
P. S. *Waverley*
from 1947 to the present

Published by Mainline & Maritime Ltd, 3 Broadleaze, Upper Seagry, near Chippenham, SN15 5EY
Tel: 07770 748615 www.mainlineandmaritime.co.uk orders@mainlineandmaritime.co.uk
Printed in the UK

Front Cover: *Columba* (1878) leaving Dunoon on 31st August 1934.
Frontispiece: The image which identified the collection - *Glen Sannox* (1925) in Rothesay Bay on 4th June 1932.
Above: *Queen Mary* (1933) departing Dunoon on 8th July 1933.
Back Cover Top: *Waverley* (1899) off Kilcreggan on 1st July 1933.
Back Cover Lower: *Waverley* (1947) in Rothesay Bay on 17th June 1947 (image by Robin B Boyd).

CONTENTS

ACKNOWLEDGEMENTS

The compilers wish to thank the following for their assistance with production of this book:
- Helen Young for donating the original negatives from her father's collection
- The staff of Gourock Library for accommodating the compilers' initial discussions
- Richard Danielson, David Green and the PSPS Archive for assistance with scanning
- Jim Summers, Chairman of the Caledonian Railway Society, for valuable advice
- The late Ian Ramsay for his technical notes
- John Whittle for his preface

FURTHER READING

- Caledonian Steam Packet Co Ltd by Iain C McArthur (CRSC 1971)
- Various Books and Leaflets written by Ian McCrorie (1942 – 2019)
- Various Books dating from 1930s of the late Duckworth and Langmuir including Clyde River and Other Steamers

OBITUARY - JOHN BERNARD MacGEORGE

21.11.65. The Clyde River Steamer Club acknowledgement of his invaluable research and help in relation to Steamers, cross Channel and mail vessels has to be mentioned as he was a brilliant in instant recognition of the subject matter, his knowledge was extensive and detailed and will be sadly missed.

PREFACE

The superb images in this book are a remarkable record of Scottish steamers over the period from 1927 to 1937. Then the world was somewhat different to the one we know today. People managed somehow without the internet, social media, mobile phones or television and it would be some years before the demands of the motor car imposed significant changes to the ships and services.

Although a start had been made in providing improved homes, many occupied poor quality housing and a trip on a steamer was a chance to exchange the smoke and grime of the city for fresh sea air. Only the better off could afford holidays abroad creating the tradition of 'Ma, Pa and the weans going doon the watter at the fair' when Pa would "visit the engines" (en route to the bar!) and lunch in the magnificent dining saloons would be a real treat.

In those days, on the sail from Glasgow, passengers could see and hear the activity in the many Clydeside shipyards building some of the finest ships in the world. Sadly, like so much of our heavy industry, they have all but disappeared.

Although J. B. MacGeorge contributed some photographs of MacBrayne vessels in Hebridean waters and of ships on the River Forth, the vast majority depict Clyde Steamers, obviously his greatest interest. At that time there were a few motor vessels, driven by diesel engines but the vast majority were true steamers, powered by steam generated by coal fired boilers, including both turbine steamers and paddle steamers with paddle steamers preponderant. **Talisman**, built in 1935, introduced a new concept for she was a paddler powered by electricity from generators driven by diesel engines, a precursor of today's hybrid ferries.

The book will bring back many happy memories, firstly for those who were around during the period covered and for many others recalling later periods as many of the ships and services continued for several years. The last to retire were PS **Caledonia** in 1969, TS **Duchess of Hamilton** in 1970, TS **King George V** in 1974 and TS **Queen Mary** in 1977. PS **Caledonia** became a floating restaurant on the Thames until, sadly, destroyed by fire. TS **Queen Mary** followed suit but has returned to the Clyde to undergo extensive restoration in preparation for a new life as an educational, heritage, conference and function centre. She will be well worth a visit when the restoration is complete.

In addition, we are indeed fortunate that, thanks to the determined efforts of those who have preserved that icon, PS **Waverley**, it is still possible to experience the delights of a trip on a paddle steamer similar to that enjoyed by the passengers on the earlier steamers featured in this book.

John Whittle

John Whittle was Manager of The Caledonian Steam Packet Company from 1969 – 1973, and General Manager of Caledonian MacBrayne from 1973 – 1983.

Waverley (1899) in Loch Long 27th August 1932. The magnificent **Waverley** speeds through the tranquil waters of Loch Long on her homeward journey from her daily sailing to Arrochar. After having allowed her passengers an hour on shore she was due to leave at 1410 and make her way to Lochgoilhead before returning to Craigendoran via Blairmore and Kilcreggan. At Craigendoran she would put ashore her Glasgow and local traffic then load those passengers returning from the Three Lochs tour plus evening commuters and then set out again, via Helensburgh to Kilcreggan, Kirn, Dunoon, Innellan, Craigmore and Rothesay thereafter providing a sailing back to her base. Having collected LM&SR passengers at Gourock on the way out she would put them ashore at Kirn to return on any LM&SR sailing to Gourock. A busy life indeed! In 1933 she was fitted with a forward deck shelter which sadly served to slow her down.

INTRODUCTION

On 4th July 2019 Mrs Helen Gillies arrived at the Waverley Office in Glasgow with a large box of material which she thought might be of use for fundraising towards new boilers for the old ship. When the box was opened by Gordon Wilson and Iain Quinn of the Scottish Branch of the Paddle Steamer Preservation Society they found, to their delight, that it contained hundreds of old slides of Scottish steamers taken in the 1920s and 1930s. Although initially the photographer's name was not known, by chance it was spotted that the 1972 edition of *Clyde River and Other Steamers* contained one of the images, credited to J. B. MacGeorge. All the old slides were in individual envelopes with copious details in the same handwriting, so it seems certain that all had been taken by J. B. MacGeorge, that they had been presented to Helen's father, John Young, upon Mr MacGeorge's death and that eventually they had fallen to Helen upon the death of her father. It was quickly realised that the collection was a veritable treasure trove of material of great significance and the decision was taken that they should be shared with the wider public in the form of a book.

Sadly, not a lot is known about the photographer. John Bernard MacGeorge was born in Glasgow in June 1897 to Bernard Buchanan MacGeorge and Ellen MacGeorge nee Whigham of 10 Woodside Crescent, Glasgow. They had been married in Ayr on December 4th, 1888. The young John was born into a prosperous background, his father being listed as a stockbroker by profession. One imagines John Bernard had a conventional childhood in a middle class professional family during which he became interested in Clyde Steamers and the joy of photography which he was able to combine together to our benefit. He followed his father into the profession of stockbroker and resided in a handsome villa in Wemyss Bay, an excellent location for a man of his interests. He was appointed a Burgess of the Trades House of Glasgow on 23rd October 1936, and remained a bachelor all his life. He passed away in Larkfield Hospital, Greenock, on 21st November 1965.

When the contents of the box were collected together it was found that there were over 500 slides, taken in the period from the late 1920s up to the outbreak of the Second World War. Most of them were taken on the Clyde in locations stretching from the river down into the firth, into its many lochs and ports and encompassed such parts as Craigendoran, the Gareloch, Gourock, the Cowal piers, Rothesay, the Kyles of Bute, Arran, Inveraray and Campbeltown. In addition, there were slides of steamers on Loch Lomond, at Oban and Kyle of Lochalsh, Islay, Dundee and Granton on the Forth. The period in which they were taken was one of profound change which witnessed the end of one distinct era in steamer history and the beginning of another. Thus, there are photographs of vessels built in the Golden Years of the late Victorian era and the beginning of the twentieth century when competition between the various railway fleets was intense while the smaller independent owners kept going and eventually began to add to their fleets. These years witnessed great technological change, the most profound element being the introduction of the turbine steamer, beginning with **King Edward** in 1901. This world was brought to a shuddering end by the calamity that was the Great War and its immediate aftermath was a period of retrenchment and a rearrangement of services, owners and vessels.

After a period of marking time, the mid 1920s began a process of gradual modernisation which saw some new vessels being introduced. However, the decade ended with the shock of the Wall Street Crash and the Great Depression. While this led to great hardship and suffering and the birth of an ominous new political reality it was paradoxically a great time for those still in work and for shipowners. Thus, passengers began to flock back to the Clyde and owners were able to take advantage of low building and running costs to introduce a whole array of new vessels and the 1930s witnessed the introduction of the marine diesel engine, the diesel electric paddle vessel and the concept of one class cruising vessels. As new vessels were introduced the older vessels were withdrawn and this process provided great excitement for the steamer enthusiast of the day. It was this transition that Mr MacGeorge copiously recorded with his camera.

When it came to deciding which slides should be included in the book we had great difficulty making decisions and many were the arguments over what should be in and what should be left out. We used the parameter of trying to use the slides to tell the story of the period. Thus, we included as many of the pre Great War vessels as we could and then followed this with the vessels of the new age that began in the late 1920s and really took off in the 1930s. However, we also tried to pick shots that reflected the everyday and the mundane as well as those that were truly unique. To those that lived through the period many of our choices would have seemed pedestrian; they reflected the everyday and depicted scenes that would probably not have earned a second glance. However, there will be virtually nobody alive today who was active during the period with the result that all we have chosen will appear both splendid and magical. To our generation the sight of the 1934 **Mercury** sailing across Rothesay Bay is a tremendous sight as is **Columba** at Tarbert, **King George V** at Inveraray and **Davaar** at Campbeltown. However, we have also included more unusual and historical shots such as **Lochness** leaving her builder's yard to go on trials, **Fusilier** and **Glencoe** at Portree, **Minard** and **Ardyne** passing off Toward and **Lochiel** alongside at Bruichladdich. We have also tried to portray most of the vessels that were in service in the period, ranging from **Wee Cumbrae**, via **Columba** to the magnificent **Duchess of Hamilton** and not forgetting the vessels of the Clyde and Campbeltown Co. We have also tried to include as many calling points and locations as possible to reflect the various duties that the vessels undertook. Where possible, we have also tried to include shots that show vessels in slightly different guises from the remembered, such as the 1896 **Jupiter** with a deck cargo of sheep at Princes Pier. It may seem from the selection that some vessels appear to be more favoured than others. However, this reflects the contents of the collection – Mr MacGeorge seemed to have taken more shots of some vessels than others.

Although the bulk of the photographs are from the Clyde other areas have also been included to hopefully provide scenes that will not be well known to the modern enthusiast. Thus, we have photographs taken on Loch Lomond in winter as well as summer and scenes at Oban and some points north. Uniquely, we have also managed to include views from the Forth and the Tay. These range from the normal scenes at Granton and Dundee to the rare with shots taken on board **Fair Maid** when she relieved during the winter on the Granton to Burntisland service.

We hope that this book tells a story, on the one hand presenting you the reader with a collection that tells the story of the steamers in the period while also giving an indication of what life was like on the vessels at the time. We felt that we should do more than just produce a series of fascinating photographs of all the vessels. Instead, we wanted to give a feel for what life was like between the wars. We wanted in our selection to show modern enthusiasts and non enthusiasts alike the story of a bygone age when paddle steamers and turbines swarmed across the Clyde to a myriad of towns and villages in an almost endless procession. Although all the participants afloat and ashore did not realise it at the time it was a period on borrowed time which was soon to be swept away.

DC, November 2020

Talisman **(1896) approaching Rosneath 1st March 1930.** *Talisman*, like *Kenilworth*, was a vessel that was utilised all year round on the L&NER's coast services. While normally serving Dunoon and Rothesay she was also used to relieve *Lucy Ashton* to allow the older vessel time off for her annual overhaul. Thus, out of necessity, a larger vessel was employed on the loch run when traffic was at its scarcest. Although most Clyde towns and villages had their own pier they were not always situated close to the community they served and this was true of Rosneath where passengers had quite a walk to get to and from the village. *Talisman* served her owners well in a career that spanned almost 40 years. She was withdrawn and scrapped in 1934 but her name lived on in a new vessel commissioned in 1935.

***Lady Clare* (1891) being broken up at Dumbarton April 1928.** In this sad shot an old Clyde lady is meeting her inevitable end. Even by NBR standards *Lady Clare* was a basic vessel and had a life virtually unknown to most Clyde residents and enthusiasts. She was built as a simple ferry and spent her relatively short Clyde life sailing either to the Gareloch piers or to Greenock. She was withdrawn in 1906 during one of the periodic "cullings" the railways had when times were hard and was sold to Ireland where the Moville Steamship Co. employed her on Lough Foyle and for tendering. Apart from war service as a minesweeper based in Belfast she remained there until she was sold for breaking up in 1928. Latterly the political division of Ireland had inhibited her earning a living. Interestingly, part of her after saloon was bought from the breakers to be converted into a houseboat but this idea appears not to have been carried through.

Lady Clare (1891) at Dumbarton April 1928. As time passes most ships arrive at the point where they are considered not worth keeping in service and they invariably end up in a ship breaking yard where they are cut to pieces and all parts are sold off for whatever money the breakers can obtain. Here, the ***Clare*** has obviously not been in the yard for long as she is substantially still whole. However, her port telegraph has gone and work has begun in dismantling the port paddle casing. Ashore, an ancient steam crane is fired up to take the cut up pieces ashore where they will be taken apart and sorted for subsequent sale. If the vessel had been famous the breakers would invariably have done a roaring trade in selling off bits to the public but for lesser lights like ***Lady Clare*** public interest would have been minimal. So ended the life of one of the Clyde's lesser lights.

***Kylemore* (1897) sailing down the river with Ardmore Point in the background.** In this photograph *Kylemore* is paddling down the river with what looks like an exceedingly large crowd on board. The Williamson management were ever aware of possibilities for adding to their traffic and raising revenue and one such way was advertising *Kylemore*'s return cargo sailing as an afternoon cruise to Dunoon and Rothesay. Time ashore was available at the former but at Rothesay the passengers had to quickly change to a vessel returning to Bridge Wharf. Another opportunity was the various Glasgow holidays when the whole fleet was utilised in special sailings from Bridge Wharf and this gave *Kylemore* the opportunity to become a regular excursion vessel for a short period. Just to add to her fun, she was frequently advertised for evening cruises out of Rothesay!

Lord of the Isles* (1891) off Greenock May 1927.** *Lord of the Isles* was one of the most famous and luxurious steamers on the Clyde. She had been built for the Glasgow to Inveraray service on which she provided a round trip each weekday. She was a major rival to MacBrayne's ***Columba and their daily races were watched by thousands. The arrival of the turbine steamers on the Inveraray route substantially killed off her trade and she was eventually bought by Williamson for further use. She was relegated to sailings such as a cruise Round Bute and remained as such until 1927. She was chartered by MacBrayne in 1928 for their Lochgoilhead cruise but such were her running costs she was withdrawn after that season. In this shot she is devoid of passengers which suggests she is about to run trials after her annual overhaul. She retained the distinctive funnel colour of red with black top and two narrow white lines and burnished copper steam pipes throughout her life.

Jupiter* (1896) arriving at Princes Pier 6th July 1930.** The former "pin-up" of the G&SWR fleet is coming alongside at the G&SWR's former Clyde headquarters on a Saturday afternoon preparatory to leaving again at 1430 for Gourock and the Kyles of Bute piers including Ormidale. During the morning she undertook a sailing from Princes Pier to Rothesay followed by a return sailing as far as Gourock. Once unloading was over she then sailed up to Princes Pier to begin the cruise. By 1930 Princes Pier was slowly having its service reduced in favour of Gourock but the process took a remarkably long time and it was actually the Second World War that eventually finished off regular sailings from Princes Pier. In the immediate postwar years all it could boast was one sailing a day to Rothesay and the Kyles and even that disappeared after a few years. ***Jupiter had the misfortune to be due out at the same time as ***Duchess of Montrose*** but it is a safe bet to wonder which of them got to Gourock first! Behind ***Jupiter*** is a Clyde Shipping Company tug awaiting passage up the river.

Duchess of Montrose* (1930) berthing at Princes Pier 26th July 1930.** The magnificent ***Duchess of Montrose is shown coming alongside at Princes Pier in her first year in service. With Captain James Riddell at the telegraph and the crew in position to put ashore the ropes she is about to berth. She was based at Gourock and only appeared at Princes Pier on Saturday afternoons when she carried out an afternoon cruise Round Ailsa Craig which was due to depart at 1430 and arrive back at 2110. She had no rostered sailings on Saturday mornings and was due to lie alongside at Gourock, but, on peak dates, she was sometimes used to ease the forenoon pressure at Gourock or Wemyss Bay. On the other days of the week passengers for her were conveyed from Princes Pier on ***Duchess of Argyll*** to Gourock to join her there. Her arrival on the Clyde made big inroads into Williamson's traffic to Campbeltown and Inveraray.

***Comet* (1905) and *Duchess of Argyll* (1906) off Princes Pier 8 September 1930.** Some would call this photograph a combination of the sublime and the ridiculous. In the foreground MacBrayne's motor vessel **Comet** is coming alongside the pier to undertake her daily sailing to Lochgoilhead which was due to leave Greenock at 0900 and Gourock at 0935. Round the year she was rostered to make one round trip and was due back from this in mid-afternoon. During July and August she lay at Lochgoilhead overnight thus making it possible for anyone of a mind to commute daily to and from Glasgow. In the background **Duchess of Argyll** is on the 0840 sailing from Princes Pier to Arran via the Kyles and is making her way to Gourock, her first call. Whatever the merits of each vessel, both were carrying out important duties to the communities they served and have their own individual places in Clyde Steamer history. In the background are the Rosneath Peninsula and the hills surrounding Loch Long and Loch Goil.

***Kylemore* (1897) turning into Princes Pier September 1931.** Throughout her Williamson career **Kylemore** was employed on their Rothesay to Glasgow cargo and passenger service. For this, she berthed overnight at the inside of Rothesay Pier and left every morning at 0815 for Innellan, Dunoon, Kirn and Princes Pier before continuing up the river to Renfrew, Govan and Bridge Wharf. On most days she would load more cargo and livestock than she would passengers and large sacks are seen here piled up under the bridge. However, on Saturdays, the sailing terminated at Princes Pier and she was then utilised as a tender to transatlantic liners lying off Greenock. In this shot she is turning round into Princes Pier suggesting it is a Saturday. Note the large steering wheel on the bridge.

Duchess of Rothesay* (1895) arriving at Princes Pier 2nd April 1932.** Most pictures of ***Duchess of Rothesay show her sailing on the firth during summer weather conditions but she was also employed on the winter services. For such service the opening on the main deck forward and the windows in the forward saloon were covered over with heavy metal shutters to protect them from the heavy seas frequently encountered on the firth during winter. As it was April the Spring timetable would have been in operation and in this photograph she would be returning to Princes Pier around 1620 from the forenoon Kyles sailing. By her appearance she has been in service for months and would soon undertake a visit to a local slip to be cleaned, repainted and have the shutters removed before embarking on summer duties.

Caledonia* (1889) pulls away from Princes Pier 26 August 1933.** Taken in her last year of service, we see ***Caledonia leaving Princes Pier, ostensibly according to her fanboard for Gourock but thereafter to Kilcreggan and the Holy Loch piers. In her early days she had made a name for herself operating from the CR's new terminal at Gourock to Dunoon and Rothesay but in the first decade of the twentieth century she was switched to the Holy Loch service where she became well known and very popular with regular traffic. Originally, the G&SWR vessels competed with the CSP on this service as they did on all others but by the end of the first decade of the new century a pooling arrangement between the companies to avoid wasteful competition had meant that the two services were amalgamated into one which led to ***Caledonia*** adding Princes Pier to her itinerary. Several months after this photograph was taken the old ship was withdrawn and sold for scrap at Barrow. Her passing was mourned by many.

Isle of Arran **(1892) and** *Duchess of Rothesay* **(1895) pass off Princes Pier 2nd April 1932.** This photograph illustrates a fascinating combination of vessels with *Isle of Arran* and *Duchess of Rothesay* passing with the Canadian Pacific liner *Duchess of Richmond* at anchor and a Clyde puffer sailing upriver in the background. This interesting combination shows *Duchess of Rothesay* about to turn to berth at Princes Pier while *Isle of Arran* meanders her way past. The presence of the liner and the time of day suggests that *Isle of Arran* is on tender duty to the liner and is about to turn towards her to go alongside. Canadian Pacific liners called off Greenock at least once a week throughout the year and required the use of a tender as they were too large to berth alongside themselves. This provided Williamson-Buchanan with a profitable income and during the winter months the vessel they normally employed on this duty was *Isle of Arran*.

Lucy Ashton **(1888) arriving at Princes Pier 14th July 1934.** As well as her regular duty of linking the ports on the Gareloch to Helensburgh and Craigendoran, *Lucy Ashton* operated a regular service between Craigendoran and Greenock. Normally four or five sailings were provided on weekdays with three on Sundays during the summer timetable with a reduced timetable during the winter. The bulk of the traffic using the service were day trippers seeking a day to experience the delights of Helensburgh or others seeking a sail on the Gareloch. Sometimes traffic was bound for the West Highland line at Craigendoran. However, there was also a regular traffic composed of commuters working on either side, businessmen and commercial travellers and some desiring to indulge in the shopping delights of Greenock. The service continued after the war, albeit to Gourock but the traffic tailed off to a fraction of what Lucy had carried before the war.

Jupiter **(1896) alongside at Princes Pier September 1931.** As well as her cruising duties out of Princes Pier and the coast resorts *Jupiter* was also engaged in normal service runs which started with a sailing at 0805 from Innellan to Dunoon, Kirn, Hunters Quay and Kilcreggan direct to Princes Pier where she was due at 0903 and she is seen here on completion of the sailing which included this day carrying a flock of sheep. To accommodate them deck seats, deck mats and assorted barrows have been piled up at the bow to free some deck space for them. Once loaded they were penned in by using an assortment of livestock pens and gangways and would be unloaded after all the passengers had gone ashore. Once off the deck would be hosed down to clear any mess and the seats put back into position. As she was due to leave again at 0930 the crew would have to have worked very quickly. All in a day's work on a Clyde steamer!

Kylemore **(1897) berthed at Princes Pier March 1933.** Although the sight of *Kylemore* alongside at Princes Pier was an everyday event this particular photograph is significant because of the date it was taken. Williamson-Buchanan sailings usually got underway for the season in April. The fact that this shot was taken the previous month suggests she was on tender duty. This involved the vessel going alongside the liner at the Tail of the Bank and taking on board passengers from the larger ship bound for the special train to Glasgow. Once this was done then it would be the turn of passengers heading for Canada to board her. The fact that there appears to be quite a crowd on the pier watching proceedings gives credence to this theory. They would either be welcoming home relatives or else seeing them off to a new life across the Atlantic. Note the seaman nonchalantly sitting on the rail at the lifeboat!

Lucy Ashton (1888) arriving at Craigendoran 2nd July 1932. To put it mildly, the *Lucy* is somewhat busy in this photograph! Her wake demonstrates that she has come across the Tail of the Bank from Greenock with what must have been a near capacity complement of passengers and she is positively labouring under the weight. Such a scene suggests this could have been Greenock Fair Saturday, the start of the town's annual holiday period and all vessels sailing from Princes Pier that day would have left carrying nearly their complement of day trippers and holidaymakers. For most of those on the *Lucy* their ultimate destination would have been Helensburgh where they would have enjoyed the delights of a major holiday resort. Some more adventurous souls would have walked the length of the pier station to reach the main line platforms and joined a train on the West Highland Line bound for Fort William. The Second World War put paid to the Greenock service and saw it being transferred to Gourock.

Jeanie Deans (1931) and *Waverley* (1899) at Craigendoran 12th May 1931. In this atmospheric photograph one can feel the excitement at the beginning of a new season when newly overhauled vessels have returned to their base to undergo final preparations before beginning their season. However, special excitement would have been evoked by the presence of *Jeanie Deans*, newly delivered from her builders. In her original condition *Jeanie* was built without a forward deck saloon and with rather short funnels, the latter of which proved a nuisance by depositing soot on the heads of passengers on the afterdeck. This was remedied in the winter of 1931-32 when they were heightened. At the other side of the pier lies *Waverley*, the previous pride of the fleet. She was no doubt irked at being demoted to the Rothesay and Kyles sailings but could still show the young upstart a clean pair of heels when required! The building of the new vessel demonstrated to the world that the L&NER were determined to hold their own against the gathering onslaught from the LM&S fleet.

Kenilworth (1898) and **Lucy Ashton** (1888) leaving Craigendoran September 1931. Both steamers have left the pier virtually together having made the same train connection at Craigendoran. On the left is **Kenilworth** heading for the Cowal coast while **Lucy Ashton** heads for her Gareloch home. The lack of fanboards being displayed on the former suggests the time is around 1630 and that she is heading for Kilcreggan, Hunter's Quay and Kirn while the latter will end up at Garelochhead. There should also have been a third vessel leaving for Dunoon and Rothesay but to the left can be seen a vessel speeding towards Craigendoran and this could possibly be **Waverley** returning late from Arrochar to undertake this sailing. No doubt after a fast change of passengers she would have set off for her destination. Scenes like these were common at most of the Clyde railheads as each company vied to get their passengers to their destinations before the others. Happily, although on a smaller scale, this scene can still be observed at Gourock with small ferries leaving for Kilcreggan and Dunoon from the same train connection.

Lucy Ashton (1888) in close up, Craigendoran 1932. Apart from being built in Rutherglen, **Lucy Ashton** was always regarded as a nondescript vessel pottering away in the background and in fact was almost withdrawn in the early years of the twentieth century. However, she outlived all of her contemporaries and paddled across the Clyde for 60 years. Undoubtedly her finest hour was the Second World War when she maintained the L&NER's one ship service on her own with only 10 days out of service throughout the whole conflict. She even had the honour of having the Clyde's first female purser, Jean Vickery! For most of her career she was associated with the Gareloch service and the ferry service to Greenock. The former was not renowned for being passenger intensive so the large crowd disembarking at Craigendoran suggests she has arrived from Greenock Princes Pier. The amusing story is told of several drunken passengers embarking for Greenock and taunting the police at Craigendoran only to be met by their counterparts at Greenock!

Talisman (1896) leaving Craigendoran 2nd July 1932. *Talisman* was built as a ferry class paddler to operate all the year round the NBR's basic services to Dunoon and Rothesay from which she rarely deviated throughout her entire career, except for the period of the Great War when she was called up to the colours. Unlike their South Bank counterparts the NB did not believe in wasting money and she was fitted with single crank machinery. A feature of operations at Craigendoran was that steamers were regularly berthed facing bow out to enable them to get a fast getaway rather than waste valuable time reversing out then having to turn round to face down the firth before they could increase speed. For all routes other than that to the Gareloch the NB were at a major geographical disadvantage and every means had to be employed to attempt to beat their CSP and G&SW rivals to the piers. Despite the grouping of 1923 the rivalry continued and if anything increased until the late 1930s when the L&NER was forced to concede that the LM&S fleet had finally gained supremacy.

Jeanie Deans (1931) departing Craigendoran 2nd July 1932. In 1931 the L&NER decided to build a vessel designed to compete directly with the CSP cruising turbine *Duchess of Montrose* and *Jeanie Deans* was the result. Most unusually she was built by Fairfield rather than by Inglis because the latter felt that the L&NER's stipulations were impossible to attain and therefore did not bid. The end result nevertheless was an outstanding vessel that became immediately popular with the travelling public. As built she looked somewhat old fashioned and looked stranger still in 1932 when her original stumpy funnels were raised by different heights. She was originally employed on her owner's premier service to Lochgoilhead and Arrochar but from 1932 she provided a variety of long distance cruises to such destinations as Round Arran, Ayr and Girvan. This shot shows her steaming out of Craigendoran in a determined fashion to challenge her South bank rival for the cruise crowds. Sadly the L&NER's optimism for these cruises was never quite realised and by the end of the 1930s *Jeanie Deans* found herself again sailing to Lochs Goil and Long.

***Talisman* (1935) on her first visit to Craigendoran 15th June 1935.** In 1935 the L&NER threw caution to the wind and built the Clyde's first diesel electric paddle vessel. Her motive power consisted of a motor that received power from 4 English Electric diesel engines. The selling point of this type of installation was that it greatly reduced running costs, very important on the winter service. She is newly arrived at Craigendoran and officials on the bridge are being given a lecture on the finer points of her construction. Note the foredeck which is piled high with stores. For the first few years the vessel proved her worth to her owners by sailing most efficiently. Sadly however problems began to affect her from 1937 onwards and these culminated in her coming to a halt in 1939 due to a crankshaft failure. It was discovered that many of her problems were caused by initial design faults but for her owners enough was enough and she was laid up to early 1940. With the declaration of war she was taken in hand and was repaired and, ironically, thanks to the modifications carried out, she behaved impeccably while on Government service.

Lucy Ashton* (1888), *Kenilworth* (1898) and *Marmion* (1906) at Craigendoran 12th March 1936.** By 1936 the L&NER found themselves fighting a losing battle against the might of the LM&SR and decided to try and make their vessels more appealing by giving them a new colour scheme of grey hulls and white upperworks. The first vessel to be so treated was ***Kenilworth and in this illustration she has just arrived at Craigendoran. However she was photographed again several days later in Bowling Harbour which suggests that she had been hurried out to cover for another vessel and then returned to dock to finish her overhaul. A ladder has been placed up her funnel, no doubt for cleaning and painting purposes. Just as MacBrayne found several years earlier the Clydeside public did not like grey hulls and they complained vigorously. However, unlike MacBrayne, the L&NER took no notice of the complaints and the colour scheme remained until replaced by a more sombre grey in 1939.

Kenilworth* (1898) and *Lucy Ashton* (1888) lying in Bowling Harbour 15th March 1936.** For many years Bowling Harbour served as the winter quarters for a large number of Clyde steamers but by the 1930s it was mostly restricted to vessels of the L&NER Clyde fleet. On the left is ***Kenilworth wearing the new colour scheme of the L&NER fleet introduced that year while to the right is ***Lucy Ashton*** still in the old colours which she continued to sport during her Spring sailings. An earlier photograph showed both vessels at Craigendoran on 12 March so this shot demonstrates that the problem at Craigendoran is over and ***Kenilworth*** has returned to dock to finish her overhaul. She has been joined by ***Lucy Ashton*** which has been relieved in service and has come upriver to Bowling to begin her own overhaul which would involve a visit to the slip at Pointhouse for survey and repainting. Note that the ladder is still attached to ***Kenilworth***'s funnel!

Waverley* (1899) approaching Helensburgh July 1929.** On a lovely summer's evening we see the flagship of the L&NER fleet sailing from Craigendoran to Helensburgh. We can note from her wake how she has changed course in order to line herself up to take Helensburgh pier no doubt after having left Craigendoran bow first. In the normal scheme of things she should not have been anywhere near Helensburgh which suggests that she is making the unusual call on an evening cruise. In order to facilitate this, rosters would be reordered so that another vessel could have taken ***Waverley's normal evening sailing to Rothesay while she in turn would probably have taken the run at 1635 from Craigendoran to Hunter's Quay and Kirn. Her actual evening cruise would pick up at several piers, sometimes including the Gareloch piers, and then proceed down the firth sometimes reaching as far as the Arran coast. Just behind her stern can be discerned another vessel heading into Craigendoran.

King Edward* (1901) approaching Helensburgh August 1929.** On a dull, overcast evening we can observe the Clyde's pioneer turbine steamer ***King Edward slowly approaching Helensburgh ready to take up an evening cruise. Evening cruises, whether organised by the owners or charters organised by special parties, were a popular and lucrative feature of the interwar period. Relatively cheap to run they were capable of raising a substantial amount of revenue. For the White Funnel turbines Helensburgh was a lucrative calling point as it gave them access to North Bank traffic from as far away as Clydebank and the Glasgow area. However, such cruises were extremely strenuous on the crew. By the time the vessel had returned to all the pick up points then settled down for the night it could be midnight before the crew got to their beds and they would be up again at 0500 for another day.

King George V* (1926) approaching Helensburgh August 1929.** As well as the normal day sailings a very successful source of revenue for steamer companies was the provision of evening cruises which could take passengers as far as Arran or Loch Fyne. While most such cruises tended to focus on the railheads and main piers smaller piers also got their share of evening cruises leading to the turbines being seen in for them strange places. Thus ***King George V is pictured coming into Helensburgh on such a sailing. Day cruises were relatively expensive compared to modern times which deterred many from using them. However, evening cruises could take them a relatively good distance at half the price. With entertainment regularly provided such cruises were tremendously successful. When built ***King George V*** had been fitted with Yarrow water tube boilers but they were not considered a success and several crew were killed in 1927 after an accident in the stokehold. In 1929 she was fitted with Babcock & Wilcox boilers while navy tops were fitted to her funnels.

Kenilworth (1898) off Mambeg April 1929. Although better known on the Craigendoran to Rothesay service *Kenilworth* was considered to be an all year round vessel and could be found on other routes as required. Thus, she found herself relieving on the Gareloch service while *Lucy Ashton* was off for repairs or annual overhaul. Sailings to the Gareloch originated literally at the beginning of steam navigation on the Clyde and were operated by various different companies. When the NBR started Clyde sailings in 1865 they eventually settled for the mundane local services rather than their original grand plan of sailing to the Kyles and Loch Fyne and they instituted a service to the Gareloch in 1869 using the *Carham*. By the 1890s they had the regular all the year round route to themselves and operated it as a stand alone service but, after the departure of *Lady Clare* in 1906, it was combined with the ferry service to Greenock.

Talisman (1896) at Rosneath April 1927. During another spell of relief work *Talisman* is seen alongside at Rosneath. Given that she is berthed port side to at the pier she has probably called on her way from Craigendoran to the loch piers. The first point of interest is the almost complete lack of passengers both on the vessel and standing on the pier. The second is the fact that she has got two planks running from her forward sponson on to the pier and they are being used to facilitate the unloading of what appears to be several large crates, presumably on a cargo trolley. This was repeated at piers all over the firth where seamen and pier staff laboured to move all sorts of cargo between ship and shore. This would not be an easy job at the best of times but if the tide was low it proved to be an exceedingly difficult task to undertake. Also of interest is the fact that the walkway on to the pier is of metal construction and not of the more usual wood.

Lucy Ashton (1888) alongside at Mambeg September 1929. When one considers the NBR and L&NER's Gareloch service the vessel most associated with it was ***Lucy Ashton*** which operated it from early in the twentieth century up to its final demise in 1944. A sailing on the loch was a must for anyone who enjoyed a trip in pretty scenery that encompassed a large number of calls. Setting off from Craigendoran the service consisted of calls at Helensburgh, Rhu, Rosneath, Clynder, Shandon, Rahane Ferry, Mambeg and Garelochhead where the vessel lay overnight. In one sense in providing this service the L&NER was competing with itself as it provided a local service on the West Highland Line from Craigendoran to Arrochar which stopped at several of the villages on the northeast side of the loch. As time progressed after the Great War the traffic on the steamer fell and piers closed with the result that the last loch pier still in operation was Clynder which finally surrendered to the inevitable and closed in 1944 thus ending a historic service.

Lucy Ashton at Garelochhead 12th February 1928. ***Lucy Ashton*** is pictured lying alongside her base of Garelochhead between sailings. To modern eyes it seems incredible that in such a short distance there should be so many calls but it reflected the virtual absence of any road transport to many of the Clyde communities. The only way for people or goods to be transported in and out of the large number of villages dotted around the firth was by steamer which meant that a large fleet of vessels had to be so employed. Change only began to happen in the early 1930s when buses made their appearance and began to challenge the domination of the steamer. As well as being the base for the L&NER service Garelochhead was also visited by other members of the Clyde fleet. ***Juno*** and ***Duchess of Hamilton*** visited on day cruises from Ayr while frequent charter sailings principally on Williamson- Buchanan steamers were welcomed. On a few occasions each summer evening cruises would sail from some of the Gareloch piers all over the firth on the crack paddlers and turbines. On such occasions passengers would have to land over the decks of the dormant ***Lucy***.

Lucy Ashton **(1888) off Clynder 13th April 1936.** *Lucy Ashton* was the last Clyde vessel to retain the bridge behind the funnel and the last to have alleyways around a saloon. Clynder was the site of a rather bizarre happening when a second pier was built only several hundred feet from the original pier. Built by a speculator and called Barreman the new pier competed with the old with the steamer stopping twice in as many minutes. Eventually this odd situation was resolved when the original Clynder pier closed and Barreman was then renamed Clynder. Ironically, as well as being the newest, it was also the last operating pier on the loch. Interestingly, 1936 was the year that the L&NER railway adopted the grey hull colour scheme but ***Lucy*** is still in the old colours; she must have been the last vessel to be repainted in the new uniform.

Talisman **at Clynder March 1928.** On another spell of relieving on the Gareloch route *Talisman* can be seen slowing down to berth at Clynder towards the end of the winter service. For the railway companies winter was usually from 1 October until 31 March. The vast majority of piers were very simple affairs that consisted of a walkway from the shore connected to a berthing area for steamers. The facilities for the passengers were rudimentary to the extreme with a small building on the berthing area which had a small store and a tower for the signalling apparatus mounted on top. If they were lucky there might have been some seating for waiting passengers but not always. Clynder by the looks did not possess this luxury and the waiting passengers are having to queue in the open air - not the most enjoyable pastime in a Scottish winter!

***Duchess of Argyll* (1906) lying alongside Gourock May 1929.** The ever popular Caley turbine can be seen here lying at Gourock not in service but ready for use. Looking spruce in her new paint she is lying at Berth C with the imposing mock Tudor station building behind her. She is obviously destined to perform some duty as the famous Yellow Pennant of the Caledonian Steam Packet Company can be seen flying from her mast and some of her crew are waiting expectantly around her decks. Her mooring ropes have all been singled up but she carries no fans in her fanboards. Given that the photograph was taken in the Spring timetable she is either waiting to do a specially advertised sailing or else is ready to load a special party for a sail on the Clyde. Whatever awaits her, she would turn heads and attract admiring stares as throughout her long life she always remained a well-regarded vessel.

Comet* (1905) leaving Gourock 10th May 1930.** Full steam ahead for Lochgoilhead! Over the years the Clyde has welcomed a host of steamers of all shapes and sizes, large and small, fast and slow but has perhaps never witnessed such a strange looking vessel as ***Comet. With her small size and low hung appearance some unkind individuals called her "the Clyde's water beetle"! Loud, smelly and very basic she may have been but she performed an important function, that of maintaining a link to the villages along the shores of Loch Goil all through the year. With cargo piled up on her diminutive deck and passengers peering out of various little saloons and cubby holes, she sailed on weekdays from Princes Pier and Gourock to Carrick Castle, Douglas Pier and Lochgoilhead itself. Whatever enthusiasts thought of her, the people of the loch communities appreciated the services that she provided.

Waverley* (1899) approaching Gourock, date unknown.** As part of her daily roster the former NBR flyer can be seen slowing down to take Gourock Pier. In her heyday ***Waverley was reckoned to be one of the fastest vessels on the Clyde and more than held up the honour of the NBR in the daily races with the CSP and G&SWR owned vessels. After the Great War the building up of her bow and sundry other alterations slowed her down to a shadow of her former self but, unlike other vessels that had aged somewhat in service, she retained the appreciation of both owners and travelling public. To general regret she was withdrawn at the end of 1938 and was consigned to Bowling Harbour. However, in 1939, she was brought back out to undertake war service in which she sadly met her end returning from Dunkirk. On board she had many Clydeside soldiers who had instantly recognised the old ship. Sadly, there was heavy loss of life when she sank. The Glasgow Corporation sludge vessel ***Dalmarnock*** heads upriver in the background.

Waverley* (1899) leaving Gourock 27th August 1932.** In 1932 the L&NER decided to take on directly the immensely successful ***Duchess of Montrose and operated special day cruises to such destinations as Ayr, Round Arran and Girvan during the peak season, utilising ***Jeanie Deans***. This meant that ***Waverley*** was restored to providing the cruise to Lochgoilhead and Arrochar and thus had the honour of making the L&NER's sole call at Gourock. This put her back to what she had done for most of her life. Even though the L&NER tended to regard ***Jeanie Deans*** as their most important vessel many passengers and enthusiasts continued to regard ***Waverley*** as the crack vessel in the fleet. A friendly rivalry grew up between the adherents of both vessels and their crews and many were the regrets expressed in 1938 when the old ship was withdrawn from service.

Jeanie Deans* (1931) off Gourock June 1931.** *Jeanie Deans* gracefully pulls away from Gourock after making her daily call on her way to Lochgoilhead and Arrochar. Although a well-proportioned and fast vessel *Jeanie* was most definitely somewhat old fashioned in appearance and she brought forward mixed views from regular travellers. Although her qualities were obvious given what other new vessels that had preceded her looked like, there were some who wondered why she still bore many features of what a pre Great War vessel looked like. Her daily call at Gourock took her to the headquarters of the LM&SR steamer empire and one wonders what the CSP manager Charles Bremner made of her. Given the success of their advanced ***Duchess of Montrose introduced in 1930, did he look upon ***Jeanie*** as being something of an oddity or did her introduction to boost L&NER fortunes concern him. We will never know but, given what ***Caledonia*** and ***Mercury*** of 1934 looked like, he was certainly not influenced by her in drawing up his own plans.

Jeanie Deans* (1931) leaving Gourock June 1931.** Although the competition between the LM&SR and the L&NER was fierce in the 1930s a North Bank steamer called at the South Bank railhead once every day with the exception of Sundays. This was the vessel bound for Lochgoilhead and Arrochar which called to pick up local passengers at 1035. One call a day was obviously enough for them for on the return Gourock passengers had to change to an LM&SR vessel at Kirn. In 1931 that sailing was the preserve of the new ***Jeanie Deans, the company's flagship, and gave her an opportunity to show off to the opposition. She had been in service for barely a month and the photo gives an excellent idea of her original condition with relatively small funnels and no deck saloon which made her look somewhat old-fashioned.

Queen Alexandra (1912) pulls away from Gourock 3rd August 1931. On a beautiful calm day the packed Williamson turbine *Queen Alexandra* pulls away from Gourock bound for Lochranza and Campbeltown. Even though she has just left her berth she has already built up speed under a good head of steam as she races over to Dunoon. Dunoon had only two berths available but an L&NER steamer was due to call at 0920 on the way to Rothesay, Duchess of Argyll was due at 0925 bound for Arran, the same time as *Queen Alexandra* while *King George V* was hot on her heels at 0930 bound for Inveraray. Just to add to the fun *Kylemore* was due around 0910 bound for Glasgow. One late train or steamer could play havoc with this and the first cruise vessel to reach Dunoon could cream off the waiting crowd. Anyone who was on the prom or pier could look forward to a very entertaining 20 minutes of steamer mayhem!

Caledonia (1889) approaching Gourock 26th August 1933. *Caledonia* had the honour of being the first vessel built for the CSP in 1889 and was also the first to be fitted with compound machinery. She was also for a short time the first to be fitted to burn oil in her boilers. Although this experiment was seen as a technical success it didn't last as the cost of oil was prohibitive compared to coal. She originally was employed sailing from Gourock to Rothesay but for most of her life she operated the Holy Loch service from Gourock and then later also from Princes Pier on which she became tremendously popular with passengers. When it was announced in 1933 that she was to be withdrawn there was great regret and she was given a good send off by means of a dance in late November in Kilmun. She was broken up in Barrow, leaving the Clyde under tow in the company of *Mercury*.

Marchioness of Lorne* (1935) arriving at Gourock 21st August 1937.** During the 1930s the LM&SR seemed to be producing new vessels off an assembly line and managed to virtually rebuild their entire fleet. As well as producing crack cruising turbines they also looked to modernising the vessels involved in the bread and butter all the year round services. With ***Marchioness of Lorne they had a vessel with a good carrying and earning capacity to operate on the CSP's original service, that to the Holy Loch ports and Kirn and Dunoon. Apart from a period each day coaling at Gourock the ***Lorne*** spent about 13 hours a day calling at the Loch piers and could rack up almost 60 individual pier calls each day. Although she only infrequently wandered south of Dunoon and rarely seemed to look packed in photographs she usually managed to carry the impressive figure of over 300,000 passengers a year and turned in a small profit for her owners. In this photograph she is unusually flying her name pennant which of necessity was enormous.

Dalriada* (1926) off Gourock 21st August 1937.** A well laden ***Dalriada is pictured arriving at Gourock in the early afternoon. By this time the Campbeltown Co. had amalgamated with Clyde Cargo Steamers under MacBrayne control and she is wearing the MacBrayne red and black funnel colour. Although her sailing from Campbeltown went all the way to Glasgow most of her passengers got off at Gourock to catch a train to the city. Although the basic service was one single run a day this was increased during the summer when required and on many Saturdays she would terminate at Gourock and then give a return sailing back to the Kintyre port. She still wasn't finished and would then sail light to Glasgow arriving about midnight. The fact that she spent Sundays off duty one imagines was greatly welcomed by her hard working crew!

Ardyne **(1928) off Gourock 21st August 1937.** After completing her run to the coast *Ardyne* is pictured on her way back up the river to Glasgow. Built in 1928 she was very similar to *Minard* but was slightly shorter. No trip to the coast could be accomplished without seeing her or sister on their lawful occasions but to many people they were invisible. However, normal life in the coast towns and on the various islands would have been impossible without these vessels bringing in and taking out essential cargoes. In 1937 Clyde Cargo Steamers and the Campbeltown Co. were amalgamated under MacBrayne control into the Clyde and Campbeltown Co. With new owners came a colour change and it can be seen that she has adopted a MacBrayne red and black funnel colour. On several occasions the vessels found themselves rounding the Mull of Kintyre to pick up livestock on Islay.

Isle of Arran **(1892) pulling away from Kilcreggan 27st August 1932.** At times *Isle of Arran* was employed on the Glasgow to Lochgoilhead and Arrochar service and called at Kilcreggan on both the outward and inward sailings. Kilcreggan was a pier well used by both the LM&SR and L&NER vessels but had only the daily visit by an upriver steamer. As she pulled out of the pier the vessel was turned sharply to starboard to make for Gourock which is hidden in this photograph. Ahead of her stretches the Greenock Esplanade with its fine houses with Princes Pier station just being discernible behind the plume of smoke. The channel beyond the Princes Pier turned sharply south easterly with the result that much of Greenock is hidden and the entrance to the James Watt Dock seems much closer than it actually was.

Marchioness of Lorne **(1935) pulls away from Kilcreggan 1st June 1935.** When it was announced in 1934 that a new steamer was to be built for the Holy Loch service residents were amazed as they had expected that ***Glen Rosa*** would have been transferred to the route. This continued in 1935 when they actually saw how large ***Marchioness of Lorne*** was. With a large amount of covered accommodation she was perfect for year-round service. With calls at Princes Pier, Gourock, Kilcreggan, Cove, Blairmore, Strone, Ardnadam, Kilmun, Hunters Quay, Kirn and Dunoon the vessel rarely sailed for more than 15 minutes at a time and her crew were reckoned to be the most hardworking in the fleet! In this photograph we can see the purser on top of his office having changed the pier fanboards. A lovely looking ship of the period, she was rather cursed by a lack of speed and in service she was lucky to achieve 11 knots.

Mountaineer **(1910) arriving at Kilcreggan 13th April 1936.** Built in 1910 ***Mountaineer*** was the last paddle steamer built for MacBrayne and was distinguished by the fact that, like ***Pioneer***, she had very small paddle wheels which meant that no landing platforms were required. While an efficient vessel she sadly was not a good looking vessel, particularly in her early days when she had solid bulwarks on her promenade deck. While they did not enhance her profile they were also a nuisance as they greatly increased her windage and were replaced with the more usual railings. She was very much a "maid of all work" and was never associated with one route in particular. In summer she was always based at Oban while in winter she relieved on the Islay, Sound of Mull, Portree and Loch Goil mail services. Amusingly, she was referred to in the House of Commons as the fleet's "flapper" in 1928.

***Mountaineer* (1910) arriving at Kilcreggan 26th March 1932.** Again we see *Mountaineer* slowing to take Kilcreggan pier on the return leg of her daily sailing to Lochgoilhead. On what looks like a dull day, she seems virtually deserted. The pall of smoke at her stern suggests she has managed to beat the LM&SR Holy Loch vessel to the pier. In summer *Mountaineer* was very much part of the Oban scene but large parts of the winter were spent laid up on the Clyde. One annual event she had was on Glasgow Fair Saturday, the start of the Glasgow holidays, when she duplicated *Pioneer* on the sailing from West Loch Tarbert to Port Ellen on Islay and it was quite a sight to see both vessels struggling into the Islay port loaded to the gunwales with passengers, hampers, all sorts of luggage and a mountain of bicycles as former island residents returned home for the holiday in the company of many tourists seeking peace and quiet!

***Mountaineer* (1910) leaving Kilcreggan 13th April 1936.** One of her annual duties was to relieve the diminutive **Comet** on MacBrayne's Loch Goil service. Starting at Princes Pier she sailed to Gourock and then on to Carrick Castle, Douglas Pier and Lochgoilhead daily with the exception of Sundays. Strangely, on the inward passage she called at Cove twice a week and Kilcreggan every weekday. Thus she is seen leaving Kilcreggan at 1415 bound for Gourock and Greenock. The Lochgoilhead service was sparsely used and it was said that her arrival actually boosted traffic as many enthusiasts who would never have sailed on **Comet** turned out for her. At other times when **Comet** was off one of Ritchie Brothers' Gourock to Kilcreggan ferries replaced her which rather neatly summed up passenger demand on the route.

Waverley (1899) off Kilcreggan 1st July 1933. Here we see *Waverley* powering her way from Craigendoran down the firth. She made her way round Rosneath Point and is passing Portkill to make her first call at Kilcreggan. While virtually all LM&SR calls at Kilcreggan were made by the Holy Loch steamer virtually every passing L&NER vessel stopped at Kilcreggan, providing it with an excellent service both to Craigendoran and Dunoon and Rothesay. In 1933 *Waverley* had small saloons fitted forward and aft on the promenade deck which improved the amount of covered accommodation that she had. However, this alteration had the negative effect of adding more weight which in turn appreciably slowed her down and she lost the "greyhound" tag that she carried for most of her years. That being said, she remained an extremely popular vessel with the public.

Marchioness of Breadalbane (1890) arriving at Kilcreggan 3rd May 1930. This impressive photograph demonstrates the appeal of a paddle steamer at speed slicing through the water on her lawful occasions. As she reached the pier the master would ring down to go astern and the vessel would then, if his judgment was correct, quickly stop and come alongside the pier. One feature of Clyde timetables was always that the vessels didn't "hang about" in the sense that the timetables were constructed around the notion that vessels made brief calls at intermediate piers. Given the number of vessels in service and the fact that the majority of piers could only berth one vessel at a time this was a necessity and most piers had a signalling device to let masters know which vessel was to berth. In this shot, the *Breadalbane* is relieving her sister *Caledonia* on the Holy Loch service, an annual duty until, in late 1933, she replaced her on the run. From then *Duchess of Fife* became the relieving vessel.

The Loch Lomond steamers in winter lay-up at Balloch 29th February 1936. During the winter months the fleet tied up at Balloch and we see *Princess May* (1898) on the outside, *Prince George* (1898) in the middle and *Prince Edward* (1911) at the pier. All their deck seats have been taken ashore and caps have been placed over their funnels. Before the summer each will be slipped for painting on the adjacent slipway. The vessels carried a pretty colour scheme of grey hulls and saloons and red funnels with black tops. While looking deserted each vessel had a skeleton crew on board carrying out essential maintenance and overhaul work designed to keep the vessels in excellent condition. With each of them being out of steam and with snow on the Auchendenan hills in the background it must have been a cold job.

Princess Patricia **(1905) on Balloch Slip with** *Princess May* **behind February 1936.** Due to poor traffic returns the winter service on the loch was withdrawn after 1933 which meant that *Princess Patricia* joined her big sisters in spending the season laid up at Balloch. However, adjacent to the pier was a slip on which each vessel was taken out of the water for inspection and repair each winter. While they did not suffer from the weed and corrosion problems of their salt water colleagues on the Clyde each vessel still had to be inspected by the authorities and repainted to freshen them up for the coming season. After having lain derelict for many years the slip and its steam engine have been fully repaired and restored to their original condition in recent years.

Princess Patricia* (1905) alongside at Balloch 23rd July 1932.** In her previous life ***Princess Patricia provided a regular service between the various piers on the River Thames within London and had the rather grand name of ***Shakespeare***. When the London County Council fleet was dispersed she and her sister ***Earl Godwin*** found their way to Scotland and Loch Lomond. While the former had a long life on the loch the latter caught fire soon after arrival and probably never actually sailed for her new owners and instead spent until around the late 1920s lying, increasingly derelict, in the loch. Whatever her deficiencies in appearance, which some said were many, ***Princess Patricia*** in Loch Lomond should be considered a success and belongs to that select group of ships which are more successful when sold on by their original owners. Behind ***Princess Patricia*** can be seen Balloch Pier and Balloch Pier Station which in those days was abreast the steamer.

Princess May* (1898) at Balloch 23rd July 1932.** Balloch was the traditional home and overnight berth for the Loch steamers and alongside lies ***Princess May which is loading up for her daily run the length of the loch to Ardlui. Behind her at Balloch Pier station are the steam locomotive and coaches of the connecting train from Glasgow which would have brought most of her passengers to her. For many, it was a pleasant day out on the loch but for others the steamers provided a lifeline to the scattered communities and crofts around the loch. Some of her passengers would be looking forward to a particularly energetic day out climbing Ben Lomond for which they would leave the steamer at Rowardennan while others could be headed for a sail on the Clyde via Tarbet and Arrochar and back to Glasgow via Craigendoran. The Loch steamers were an important link in the transport chain that emanated from Glasgow by steamer around the Clyde and points north.

***Prince Edward* (1911) alongside at Balloch May 1929.** *Prince Edward* was introduced into Loch Lomond service in 1912 having unfortunately been unable to reach the loch because of low water restrictions for several months. The steamers on the loch were owned by a joint committee made up of the LM&SR and the L&NER companies and connecting trains to Balloch were run by both. Steamers on the loch were, by Clyde standards, worked very easily and most made but one round trip up to Ardlui each day with passengers being allowed plenty of time to go ashore and explore the little Highland hamlet. Connection was made each day at Tarbet with passengers carried by the L&NER vessel into Arrochar and the timetable euphemistically claimed it was but a short walk between the two villages. Sadly, they neglected to mention the long hill that was part of the walk! In the pre-war years the *Edward* was the largest of the loch vessels in service. Note the railway wagons behind her on the pier.

***Prince Edward* (1911) leaving Balloch May 1929.** *Prince Edward* sets off on her daily sailing the length of Loch Lomond from Balloch to Ardlui. In the course of the sailing passengers were conveyed virtually through Scotland in miniature with the early part of the voyage being through Lowland scenery till after Balmaha when it became more rugged leading up to the Highland mountain scenery of the north end. On this particular sailing she is, to put it mildly, lightly loaded with about only 3 or 4 souls on deck. In the background is *Prince George* (1898) which is lying idle in the loch. Not shown is *Empress* which was laid up, abandoned, to the left of *Prince George*. For those interested in paddle steamers Balloch was indeed an interesting place to visit.

***Empress* (1888) in Loch Lomond May 1929.** *Empress* was built and launched at Yoker on the River Clyde and ran her trials in the Gareloch in December 1888 but then had the misfortune to become stuck fast in the River Leven when her owners tried to get her to Loch Lomond. There she stayed for a prolonged period and it was January 1890 before she actually made it to the loch. She was one of the principal vessels in loch service but was relegated to spare, charter and relief duties in 1899 and remained thus for the rest of her career. She had the distinction of being the only Loch vessel requisitioned during the Great War but, strangely, it was for several weeks only in 1919, after the conflict was actually over! She was withdrawn from service in 1925 and thereafter languished at anchor off Balloch until being broken up in 1933. In this photograph she looks forlorn after four years of idleness.

Princess Patricia (1905) underway on Loch Lomond 9th March 1929. As a complete contrast to the other photographs of vessels in service on the loch in summer, we now have a sailing during the winter. On the Clyde the main hazards to efficient operation in winter were storms and fog. However Loch Lomond, being composed of fresh water, presented an altogether different hazard, that of ice. If the weather was cold enough for long enough it began to freeze and any vessel sailing on it had to become an icebreaker to get through. In this photograph we are on board ***Princess Patricia*** which is sailing through an ice field and what appears to be tranquil water is actually frozen. Such were the hazards and joys of winter service! We can almost imagine the cracking of the ice and feel the bitter cold!

Princess Patricia **(1905) off Luss April 1931.** As the saying goes, now for something completely different with *Princess Patricia*. While the Loch boats of the 1930s were graceful vessels the *Patricia* was small and totally different. She began life running for London County on the Thames but was bought by the Joint Committee in 1914 and proved a most useful vessel. During the summer her role was to provide short cruises from Balloch which invariably took her round the islands at the south end of the loch. During the winter she provided a service to Ardlui to cater for cargo and the few passengers that wanted to travel. She was provided with two small saloons on the lower deck and a reasonable quantity of open deck space. It is safe to assume that the latter would not have been overcrowded in January or February!

Princess May **(1898) approaching Luss June 1936.** The first stop in the circuit of Loch Lomond was the pretty village of Luss situated on its west side. Unlike some of the Loch stopping points Luss was a proper village and passengers alighting from the steamer would have been able to find amenities during their stay. This contrasted with Rowardennan and Inversnaid where, apart from one or two cottages and a hotel, there was virtually nothing. In the background can be seen Ben Lomond. *Princess May* had an interesting life in that when new she was a relief and weekend boat only. However, by the 1930s, she had been promoted to full time service with *Prince George* as her partner. Like all the custom built Loch Lomond steamers she was an attractive vessel and her fine lines were accentuated by the attractive Loch livery of grey hull and upperworks and red and black funnels. The company houseflag can be seen proudly flying at her masthead. The vessels fitted in superbly with the Loch scenery!

Prince Edward (1911) approaching Luss 16th August 1930. ***Prince Edward*** approaches the little pier at Luss with Ben Lomond in the background. On their way up the loch the steamers made calls at Luss, Balmaha, Rowardennan, Tarbet and Inversnaid. With the exception of Inversnaid all were traditional wooden piers in the Clyde style. A pleasing feature of the loch steamers was that the dining saloon was situated in the forward saloon thus affording passengers a view of the scenery while dining. Another ambitious tour carried out in conjunction with the loch steamers was the Trossachs tour in which passengers left the vessel at Inversnaid and made the short journey to Stronachlachar on Loch Katrine to join ***Sir Walter Scott*** to sail on Loch Katrine to Trossachs pier where more land transport took them to Aberfoyle and the train to Glasgow.

Prince George (1898) leaving Luss 16th August 1930. ***Prince George*** was the perfect example of a late Victorian paddle steamer with neat lines and a nicely balanced profile. With a combination of large covered saloons and a large amount of open deck space she was a perfect mix for passengers exploring Loch Lomond on any type of day weatherwise. That being said she possessed certain features that seem strange to us today including the complete lack of lifeboats bar a small craft at the stern. Also, the rope handling area at the stern was very small and the seamen standing there gives the impression of being almost squashed in. The photo suggests that this was a day of reasonable weather yet she is almost completely bereft of passengers.

Prince George **(1898) leaving Luss.** Having taken her passengers the length of Loch Lomond on her daily passage to Ardlui the vessel is now on the homeward stretch to Balloch. On first glance the vessel seems very crowded but a closer look reveals that the saloons are virtually empty. A day out on the loch presented the passenger with a variety of scenery beginning with relatively low lying land at the loch's southern end followed by a passage among the various islands that dotted the loch before entering the truly Highland scenery at its northern end. Apart from Balloch and Luss the loch's villages were small hamlets with little to them to detain passengers but that was more than made up for by the stunning scenery.

Isle of Arran **(1892) at Arrochar 27th August 1932.** Owned by Williamson-Buchanan, ***Isle of Arran*** spent her entire working life on the Clyde sailing from Glasgow, originally the Broomielaw but Bridge Wharf from 1929, "Doon the Watter" on day excursion sailings. Originally, she sailed from Glasgow to the island after which she was named, but for most of her career she made for Rothesay and the Kyles of Bute, frequently on the age-old 1100 sailing. However, from time to time she found herself visiting other corners of the Firth and this photograph shows her alongside Arrochar at the head of Loch Long. This sailing from Glasgow entailed calls at Govan, Renfrew, Gourock, Kilcreggan, Blairmore, Carrick Castle and Lochgoilhead before arriving at Arrochar where passengers were treated to an hour ashore. This sailing had been previously operated by MacBrayne utilising ***Iona*** but was taken over by Williamson-Buchanan on her transfer to Oban in 1928.

Comet (1905) leaving Lochgoilhead 5th September 1935. Over the years Clyde steamers have come in all shapes and sizes but one of the most unusual was *Comet* of the MacBrayne fleet. This little vessel was an early motor vessel of which it was said that you could hear her coming long before you saw her. A small vessel, nevertheless she had a good amount of covered accommodation. Her role was as the Lochgoilhead mail steamer and every day she would trudge from Princes Pier and Gourock to the Loch Goil villages of Carrick Castle, Douglas Pier and Lochgoilhead. While being regarded as ugly by all and ignored by most she provided an essential link from the loch without which life would have been unsustainable. As well as providing an essential service she also wandered into the cruising world and provided several evening cruises from Lochgoilhead on summer Saturdays to Dunoon. If nothing else they provided passengers with more than ample time to view the glorious scenery!

Waverley (1899) approaching Blairmore 21st August 1937. Probably the most famous and grandest vessel built for the North British Steam Packet Co. was *Waverley* of 1899. Fast, luxurious and beautiful she was the NB's answer to the flyers of the CSP and G&SW fleet and could comfortably out sail them all. The route on which she was best known was that to Lochgoilhead and Arrochar and she is seen here arriving on the return journey to Craigendoran. Many of her passengers would disembark at Arrochar and make their way over to Tarbet to sail on Loch Lomond on the Three Lochs tour which invariably meant that on the return passage the steamer was quieter than on the way out. She is seen towards the end of her Clyde career in the new colour scheme introduced by the L&NER in 1936. In the background the CSP's Holy Loch steamer *Marchioness of Lorne* can be seen crossing to Cove on the return leg of the afternoon Holy Loch cruise to Gourock and Princes Pier.

***Queen Alexandra* (1912) off Cloch August 1934.** The success of the new design of turbine steamer introduced by *King George V* and emulated by *Duchess of Montrose*, *Duchess of Hamilton* and *Queen Mary* which had a large part of the promenade deck plated up tended to make earlier steamers seem old fashioned and out of date. To counter this *Queen Alexandra* was similarly treated in 1932 and this allowed for more covered seating to be available for passengers, but internally she was still very basic compared with her turbine contemporaries. However, this was done at the cost of her appearance as the covered in area was quite small in relation to her length as compared to the more modern vessels. At the same time her third lifeboat was moved from the port top deck to aft on the promenade deck. Although some interchanging did take place *Queen Alexandra* was mostly on the Campbeltown service and was the first of the Williamson fleet to retire to winter quarters at the beginning of September each year.

***Marchioness of Breadalbane* (1890) approaching Hunters Quay 31st August 1934.** In 1934 *Marchioness of Breadalbane* was transferred to the Holy Loch service to replace her near sister, *Caledonia*. Known affectionately to steamer crews as "The Old Breadbasket" the vessel was only on the run for one season until a new vessel could be delivered in 1935 after which she was sold to Clyde ship breakers who sold her on to an English company for further service. With her demise went the last link to the first few years of the CSP. As well as being a normal stopping point for steamers Hunters Quay had the important role as emergency pier for Cowal when Dunoon, Kirn and Innellan were closed by bad weather. Although this ensured Cowal travellers got home they were invariably then faced with the delights of walking to Dunoon in inclement weather conditions!

Eagle III* (1910) and *Mercury* (1934) off Kirn 21st August 1937.** It is a Saturday afternoon and *Eagle III* has taken the 1100 sailing from Bridge Wharf bound for the Kyles of Bute. Passing her heading north is ***Mercury bound for Hunters Quay and ultimately Gourock. According to the timetable the latter was due to leave Kirn at 1325 while *Eagle* was due at 1320 so on this date *Eagle III* is running late. On Saturdays she took the 1100 sailing from Bridge Wharf while ***King Edward*** attended to the 1000. In contrast ***Queen Mary II*** had an easy time of it, not leaving until 1345. As is obvious *Eagle* has a large crowd on board which might account for her running late. With the complicated timetables of the 1930s one vessel behind time could have consequences for a number of other vessels. By 1937 Williamson-Buchanan was part of the LM&SR empire and this is reflected in her ventilators having been repainted from brown to silver.

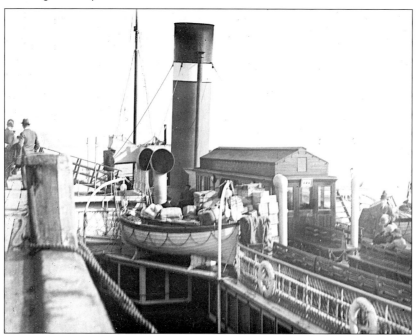

***Talisman* (1896), close up deck shot at Dunoon May 1929.** The classic Victorian paddle steamer lies at Dunoon awaiting her departure time for a sailing to Craigendoran. Like most vessels of her generation she was designed as if the Firth of Clyde was blessed with a Mediterranean climate which required the provision of large amounts of open deck space. Sadly, it is not and such vessels were a horror to travel on a terrible day if they were carrying a large load. In this particular instance this would not be a problem as she is virtually devoid of passengers. However, she is well laden with cargo and this can be seen piled high along the port side and almost encroaching on the lifeboat. This comprises a motley collection of boxes, crates, suitcases and hampers. Such was the quantity of cargo that was carried by the steamers that both the LM&SR and the L&NER had designated sailings in the morning mainly intended for cargo with an extended period alongside at Dunoon or Rothesay. One particular headache was Passengers Luggage in Advance traffic at the beginning and end of holidays and proved a nightmare to the crews who had to manhandle it on and off.

***Duchess of Argyll* (1906) at Dunoon July 1928.** The CSP turbine is pictured slowly getting underway at Dunoon around 0925 in the morning. Every weekday she left Princes Pier at 0840 and Gourock at 0908 to make her way down the firth to the East Arran ports. On the outward journey she called at Wemyss Bay, Craigmore, Rothesay and Tighnabruaich on the way to Corrie where passengers were landed by ferry, Brodick, Lamlash and Whiting Bay where she rested for an hour before returning up the firth via Garroch Head. Connections from other ports were made with passengers changing steamers at Wemyss Bay or Rothesay. On the return passengers for the Kyles of Bute changed to **Duchess of Fife** or **Mercury** at Rothesay. Until the introduction of **Duchess of Montrose** in 1930. this was the South Bank's premier day cruise, carrying a substantial total of passengers each year. Note that Dunoon pier is in its 1890s state with the tower rising from the pier itself. It was 1937 before the building was extended south and the tower placed on top.

Juno **(1898) off Dunoon July 1929.** The mighty *Juno* paddles, or struggles, towards Dunoon. This vessel was very much a "one-off" in the G&SWR fleet. Built at Clydebank, it is believed that she was intended for a South Coast operator who was unable to pay for her and she was quickly snapped up by the G&SWR. The second largest vessel in their fleet, she was heavily built and managed 19 knots on trials. Her solidity made her perfect for the Ayr excursion vessel where heavy seas could be encountered even in the middle of summer. She was given a bewildering range of cruises and could be found in virtually any part of the Firth although she was unable to call at ports in Kintyre, Loch Fyneside and the west coast of Arran. She was an immensely popular vessel and the traffic from Ayrshire increased substantially, as can be seen in this photograph where she is carrying an immense crowd. The bulk of these would disembark at Dunoon but she would then offer a cruise which would take her to Loch Long, Loch Goil or the Gareloch and she would probably add a respectable number of passengers from Dunoon to her daily total.

Kylemore **(1897) leaving Dunoon 18th August 1930.** In this photograph we can see *Kylemore* sailing between Kirn and Dunoon in the late afternoon. Even in a fleet of White Funnel paddle steamers that weren't exactly glamorous stars *Kylemore* did not stand out. She was employed by her owners principally as a cargo vessel with passengers taking second place. Based at Rothesay, her job was to perform a round trip on weekdays from Rothesay to Glasgow basically designed for cargo and livestock. What few passengers there were found themselves banished to a small area of open deck. However, her return sailing was advertised as an afternoon excursion to Dunoon and Rothesay which did attract many more passengers. In this shot cargo is stacked up round the funnel. She was also employed on evening cruises from Rothesay and nearby resorts. Such is the idea of tradition on the Clyde that her actual berth at Rothesay, Berth 1A, is to this day still referred to as the *Kylemore*'s berth.

Iona* (1864) arriving at Dunoon 16th May 1931.** By the 1930s *Iona* was a veritable survivor from an earlier age having entered her natural element almost 25 years into Queen Victoria's reign. In appearance she was very old fashioned with a canoe shaped bow, square stern, alleyways around the saloons and tall, slim funnels. She had been designed for the Royal Route from Glasgow to Tarbert and Ardrishaig but was replaced by the mighty ***Columba in 1878. Thereafter the older vessel spent her summers providing a relief service to her younger sister in the peak season to cope with the heavy traffic on the route. After the Great War MacBrayne employed her on the Glasgow to Lochgoilhead and Arrochar service but from 1927 she was based at Oban, sailing primarily on the Crinan to Fort William service in succession to ***Chevalier*** which had been wrecked in March of that year. However, each year, she returned to the Ardrishaig service in the spring and autumn when the traffic was much lighter. When she was finally withdrawn after the 1935 season she had clocked up an amazing 71 years of service, most of which was for at least six months duration each year.

King Edward* (1901) approaching Dunoon September 1931.** This photograph portrays a typical late afternoon scene on the Clyde in the 1930s. In the foreground we have a well-filled ***King Edward returning from a cruise on the firth on her way back to Glasgow. At Dunoon she would lose quite a few excursionists while gaining a probably larger number who have spent a pleasant afternoon sampling the many attractions of Dunoon while, in the background, is the L&NER's crack ship ***Waverley*** returning to her North Bank base. She has been forced to almost stop because of a lack of a berth at the pier. When one vessel departs she will quickly fill the vacant berth. In the late 1920s and early 1930s Williamson-Buchanan made a sizeable income by taking passengers on board at Dunoon, Rothesay and Largs for afternoon cruises, much to the chagrin of the LM&S who countered by employing ***Jupiter*** on similar sailings. With new vessels joining their fleet they carried the battle to their competitor up until 1936 when they finally took Williamson-Buchanan over.

King Edward* (1901) off Dunoon in 1931.** Entering service in 1901 ***King Edward was a major first and an instant sensation. She was the first commercially operated turbine steamer in the world and was very much considered an experiment. She was owned by the Turbine Steamer Syndicate and operated by John Williamson with background assistance from the G&SWR and such was her owner's caution her deck was laid out in such a way to facilitate her being converted to a paddle steamer if the experiment was unsuccessful. This it was manifestly not and her success led to similar vessels being introduced on the Clyde and elsewhere. Originally she sailed to Campbeltown and then Inveraray but, on her replacement by ***King George V***, she was transferred to sail from Glasgow, principally on the 1000 sailing to the Arran Coast. However, in 1933, the arrival of ***Queen Mary*** relegated her to the 1100 sailing to the Kyles. In this shot she is seen off Dunoon carrying a good complement of passengers.

Talisman* (1896) leaving Dunoon 1st August 1932.** This shot provides us with an evocative scene of a paddle steamer, her decks thronged with passengers, heading out from a pier on a cruise and could have been taken in many places around the British coast before the Second World War. However, rather than a cruise, ***Talisman was employed on the more mundane task of providing a basic service to the coast resorts from Craigendoran in connection with trains from Glasgow. While so employed she normally had ***Kenilworth*** as her running mate and sailed in such a way that one night would be spent alongside at Rothesay while the next would be in the Holy Loch. Unlike the LM&S Holy Loch vessel the L&NER vessel berthed overnight at Ardnadam and every morning both vessels would solemnly pass each other between Ardnadam and Kilmun. Unlike the LM&S vessel no calls were made at Blairmore or Cove. Sadly, by the 1930s, traffic from the loch to Craigendoran was virtually non-existent and the long operated service was withdrawn in 1939.

Queen Mary* (1933) approaching Dunoon 8th June 1933 in her first ten days of service.** In 1933 Williamson-Buchanan greatly enhanced their sailings out of Glasgow by the delivery of the turbine steamer ***Queen Mary. Never before had they operated such a vessel out of the city and she very quickly became popular with the travelling public. As built she was a two class ship with saloon passengers travelling forward and steerage aft. She was equipped with an impressive catering arrangement and when demand was high she could operate three different dining saloons. One peculiarity of her design was that it was impossible to walk from the bow to the stern on the main deck without passing through a toilet! Compared to the other large Clyde turbines she was not built to be very fast but rather was meant as a people carrier and could accommodate 2000 passengers when first built. She was employed on the 1000 sailing to the Arran Coast in place of ***King Edward*** and proved highly successful as such. She also proved very popular for charter sailings and provided many such cruises including evening cruises from the city throughout the season.

Columba* (1878) leaving Dunoon 1st July 1933.** One of the most majestic and stately Clyde vessels was MacBrayne's ***Columba which every day sailed all the way from the city centre to the Loch Fyne ports of Tarbert and Ardrishaig via the Kyles of Bute. In addition to local traffic she also carried those heading for more far-flung destinations such as Gigha, Islay, Jura, Oban and points north. As well as passengers she carried the mails and sundry items of cargo. On major holiday Saturdays she carried a veritable mountain of luggage ranging from the sedate leather suitcases of the middle classes to the large steel or wooden hampers of workers returning to their native island on their well-earned annual holiday. At each pier stout seamen would manhandle such items either off or on the vessel while the master stared regally down from the bridge always aware of the timetable which had to be strictly adhere to as much as possible. Woe betide any passenger considered to be taking their time!

Kylemore (1897) approaching Dunoon 1st July 1933. *Kylemore* was a vessel with an interesting history in that although she was delivered in 1897 it was actually 1908 before she sailed for the company that had ordered her! She was bought before completion by the Hastings, St. Leonards-on-Sea and Eastbourne Steamboat Co. to operate excursions from these ports. In 1904 however John Williamson brought her back to the Clyde only to then sell her to the G&SWR who renamed her *Vulcan*. However they resold her to Williamson in 1908 and she was finally able to adopt the white funnel with black top colour scheme. Quite why this merry-go-round occurred is not totally known but what is true was that Williamson was a very canny businessman and perhaps he had offers he couldn't refuse. At any rate *Kylemore* soon settled down for him and led a very successful if out of the limelight career. She was taken up to the colours in both wars and sadly was sunk by bombing off Harwich in 1940.

Duchess of Montrose arriving at Dunoon 8th July 1933. Introduced in 1930 to operate a new schedule of day cruises designed to trump the Williamson-Buchanan turbines and their inroads into LM&SR traffic *Duchess of Montrose* became one of the Clyde's most successful vessels. She was revolutionary in that she was a one-class only vessel and that class was most definitely First! With luxurious saloons, a spacious dining saloon on the main deck and plenty of open deck space for the Clyde's noted sunny weather she proved a tremendous hit with the travelling public and amply rewarded her owner's initiative. She was a good looking vessel but her looks were slightly marred in her early years by having a stump mainmast. Mercifully she acquired a full size one in 1934. Her cruises took her to such destinations as Ayr, Stranraer, Round Arran and Round Ailsa Craig and she was heavily utilised in providing evening cruises. She set new standards on the Firth and was quickly followed by a sister in 1932.

Duchess of Rothesay **(1895) arriving at Dunoon 8th July 1933.** Delivered to the CSP in 1895, ***Duchess of Rothesay*** was a fast paddler designed to best her G&SWR and NBR rivals in the daily races to Dunoon and Rothesay. Always considered one of the crack vessels in the fleet she was immensely popular with the travelling public, particularly when she replaced ***Ivanhoe*** on the Arran via the Kyles service. Unlike her predecessor she did not persist with the strange idea of being an alcohol free ship and she sailed with bars open! After the Great War she was associated with the Midday Kyles sailing from Princes Pier and Gourock till displaced by the new ***Mercury*** in 1934. Thereafter, she returned to railway connectional sailings and also provided afternoon cruises. She remained an efficient vessel all her life and, even in the late 1930s she was more than capable of maintaining 17 knots in service. In early September 1939 she had the honour of making the last CSP calls at Ormidale and Port Bannatyne.

Queen Mary **(1933) departing Dunoon 8th July 1933.** While ***Queen Mary***'s main employment was the 1000 run to the Arran Coast she was allowed a late start on Saturdays. She left Bridge Wharf at 1345 for Dunoon and Rothesay and then offered a cruise to the Kyles. This sailing during the week was normally the duty of ***Kylemore*** but she was required for tendering on a Saturday and so ***Queen Mary*** replaced her. As can be seen it was a very popular sailing! One unusual feature of the vessel was that her crew accommodation was placed at the aft end of the main deck and is represented here by the line of portholes. This allowed it to be better ventilated than other ships which endeared her to the crew. A regular sight was seeing off watch seamen and firemen seated beside the stern winch enjoying the fresh air. When this photograph was taken she had been on service for around a month but already her white water line was starting to look grubby.

***Queen-Empress* (1912) steams into Dunoon 8th July 1933.** *Queen-Empress* was a compact and handy vessel and was employed by Williamson on most of his services including relieving on the Campbeltown service during September. She tended not to be closely identified with any one service but instead took her turn on most of the sailings out of Glasgow. As well as the normal 1000, 1100 and 1330 sailings to Dunoon and Rothesay Williamson-Buchanan also had an earlier sailing from the city at 0930 which served very much as an "overflow" sailing to avoid later sailings "boiling over". On its return it normally left Rothesay at the early time of 1430 and, judging by the relative lack of passengers being carried here, it is possible that this is what the *Empress* is doing on this day. She has a very impressive smoke trail from her funnel that would leave nobody in doubt that she was a coal-burner. In the modern world that would most definitely not have been tolerated!

***Jupiter* (1896) leaving Dunoon 8th July 1933.** In this fine shot a busy *Jupiter* is pulling away from Dunoon and slowly gathering speed as she heads down the firth. In that year she sailed to Ayr on Mondays and Fridays, provided afternoon cruises on Tuesdays and Thursdays and sailed to Rothesay and the Kyles on Saturdays. Just ahead of her in the distance is *Duchess of Montrose* heading for Wemyss Bay; this suggests that it was a Saturday afternoon and the *Montrose* is heading for Ailsa Craig having left Dunoon at 1505 while *Jupiter* left the Cowal pier 5 minutes later heading for Rothesay and the Kyles. Behind the starboard paddle box can be seen a set of ferry steps suspended from a davit. This allowed her to call at Corrie although by the 1930s such calls were becoming rare for her. With the arrival of the new *Caledonia* the following year *Jupiter* found herself demoted to the Fairlie to Millport service on which she was sadly regarded as something of a plodder, a sad end for a once proud vessel.

Queen-Empress* (1912) approaching Dunoon 12th August 1933.** Once again ***Queen-Empress makes her presence felt as she steamed into Dunoon leaving an enormous smoke trail behind her. While to modern enthusiast eyes this looks wonderful it was not seen as such at the time and it can be observed that the poor unfortunates sitting on the after deck have been rendered into shadow by it while those on the foredeck are basking in glorious sunshine. Such a smoke trail was not at all popular with the local authorities and many a captain and chief engineer over the years found themselves being arraigned in the local sheriff court about producing too much smoke. When not polluting the Clyde resorts ***Queen-Empress*** was highly regarded by her owners and when she passed along with the rest of the Williamson-Buchanan fleet into LM&S ownership in 1936 she was transferred down river to operate on their services and received a yellow funnel in the process.

Kenilworth* (1898) approaching Dunoon 12th August 1933.** On a beautiful sunny day ***Kenilworth is sailing at a pace towards Dunoon on her way to Craigendoran from Rothesay. She epitomised the philosophy of the NBR who believed in building basic vessels with no frills to operate their bread and butter services to the coast. Thus she was the last single crank paddler built for service on the Clyde. That being said, she was capable of 18 knots when required. Being so fitted meant that her running costs were much less than her CSP and G&SW competitors. Another sign of economy was the lack of a sizeable dining saloon. She served her owners well and in 1938 she was bought by her builders Inglis to be broken up. Although it may seem strange that a shipbuilder should indulge in ship breaking it was a philanthropic gesture to ensure a continuity of work for their workforce at a time when orders for new ships were scarce.

Eagle III* off Dunoon 26th August 1933.** From the beginning of steamship services on the Clyde in 1812 Glasgow had been the principal port of departure for most services. However, as the 19th century progressed, the Scottish railway companies began muscling into the trade by building lines to the coast, new piers and new vessels. This, and the malodorous condition of the river which made sailing on it an ordeal, severely dented the Upriver traffic. However, by the early 20th century traffic was increasing and Buchanan built ***Eagle III in 1910 to capitalise on this. In her first season she had an alarming tendency to severely heel over but, once this was cured, she became a popular vessel sailing from the Broomielaw and then Bridge Wharf. When Williamson-Buchanan was taken over by the LM&SR in 1935 ***Eagle***'s life gained excitement and she found herself being used on railway connection sailings including two spells on the Holy Loch service.

Duchess of Hamilton* (1932) approaching Dunoon 26th August 1933.** When the plans were drawn up for building ***Duchess of Montrose it was the plan of the LM&SR to build one vessel only. However, such was her success the railway directors quickly decided to build a sister ship and thus ***Duchess of Hamilton*** appeared in 1932. Although obviously based on the one class only ***Montrose*** there were several differences such as the full length mainmast and the slightly slimmer funnels. It was decided to base her at Ayr in place of the ***Juno*** which although very popular with the travelling public was expensive to operate and getting old. The new vessel was an instant success and could visit such places as Campbeltown, the West of Arran and Loch Fyne prohibited to the older vessel. In a season she visited an amazing number of ports including such strange destinations as Ormidale and Colintraive. In the early season she also appeared on other services and on charters. Although very popular prewar her traffic figures never matched those of her elder sister.

Columba* (1878) at Dunoon August 1934.** The magnificent ***Columba briefly rests alongside Dunoon on her way back to Glasgow from the Loch Fyne ports. Even though the main Scottish holiday month was July she is well loaded with some travellers and many others having a day out on a Clyde steamer. By the 1930s the old vessel was becoming somewhat dated and old-fashioned and clearly showed that she belonged to a bygone age. Her canoe type bow with its scrolling was distinctly anachronistic by the 1930s and her bridge seemed very old fashioned as it did not stretch to the full width of the vessel. Thus, while berthing at piers the master had to stand on top of her enormous paddle box to have a clear view of the pier. On most Clyde vessels the master and mate both berthed the vessel at a pier, depending who was on watch but this practice was not used by MacBrayne where berthing was the sole prerogative of the master. For the mate it was a case of look and learn although most skippers did realise that the mate should be allowed to do it now and then to gain experience.

King Edward* (1901) pulling away from Dunoon 31st August 1934.** On the homeward leg of her cruise from Bridge Wharf we see ***King Edward gracefully leaving from Dunoon. By the end of August the annual summer rush was over but reasonable numbers of passengers would still travel as can be seen from the numbers on her deck. As it is the last day of August she would have a lot of month end traffic returning to the city. It was a great tradition of the time that families would move to a coast resort for a whole month and lodge in what we would call self catering facilities. While the mother and children enjoyed an extended break the father for part of the time would travel daily to and from his occupation and then also have his own holiday. At the beginning and end of each summer month hordes of families would be on the move and the railway companies frequently operated special sailings to accommodate the traffic. One feature would be the large number of metal boxes or baskets carried on the steamers; these contained all that the family would require for their break, including bedding and pots and pans.

Columba* (1878) leaving Dunoon 31st August 1934.** The majestic ***Columba pulls away from Dunoon on her way back to Gourock, Princes Pier and Glasgow at the end of another sailing to Tarbert and Ardrishaig. As it is the month end she is carrying a large number of returning holiday makers alongside her normal contingent of day trippers. A quick glance at her shows just how anachronistic she had become at this stage in her life. Her paddles are enormous and her deck furniture is antiquated, examples being the grandfather clock ventilators on the after deck and the ventilators at the stern. However, throughout her life, her owners did keep her up to date, such alterations being the after deckhouse and the open deck above it. On this were fitted two lifeboats taken from the ***Scout*** (1907) after that vessel was destroyed by fire. The lifeboats led an interesting life for, on the withdrawal of ***Columba***, they passed to ***King George V*** where they remained until the early 1960s. This angle allows us to see the beautiful gilt lettering and edging which continued around the hull and paddle boxes.

Iona (1864) and *Caledonia* (1934) at Dunoon September 1934. This photograph presents a fascinating view of the old and new together at Dunoon. On the left we have *Caledonia* newly introduced to service while on the right we have *Iona*, sailing in her 70th year. The shot presents a stark illustration of the changes in design in paddle steamers over the years. On the right we have the MacBrayne vessel which epitomises a steamer of the mid Victorian era, with her saloons having alleyways around them, massive paddlewheels and a square stern. On the left is 1930s modernity with full width saloons on the main deck, deckhouses on the promenade deck, a very high bridge, squat funnel and two masts. It is arguable as to which vessel is the better to travel on but to the enthusiasts of the day there would have been no doubt in their mind, *Iona* would have won hands down! However, time as always marches on and while *Caledonia* was just beginning her life, *Iona* was almost at the end of hers. Although not known at the moment the picture was taken, the veteran had only one more year to go.

Marchioness of Lorne (1935) approaching Dunoon 6th May 1935 in her first week of service. *Marchioness of Lorne* was the new LM&SR vessel of 1935 and was designed to operate the Holy Loch service. She gained a reputation as a slow coach but she did attain a speed of 15 knots on trials. As well as serving the ports around the Holy Loch she also called several times a day at Hunters Quay, Kirn and Dunoon. In the background can be seen MacBrayne's *Lochfyne* which spent her winters replacing *Columba* on the Tarbert and Ardrishaig service before being based at Oban during the summer for the Staffa and Iona service. She was the envy of all Clyde crews in that she had an enclosed wheelhouse which made her perfect for facing the winter storms. The fact that she is in the picture shows that it is around 0945 in the morning and the *Lorne* is positioning herself for a sailing at 1000 to Gourock. Both vessels are dressed overall to celebrate the 25th anniversary of the accession to the throne of King George V.

***Jeanie Deans* (1931) pulling away from Innellan July 1931.** Having briefly stopped at Innellan *Jeanie Deans* is beginning to gain speed to overtake the vessel that the photograph has been taken from. Given that she is in the inside position she will have to pass the other vessel in order to be able to round Toward Point and head towards Craigmore and Rothesay. If that was not possible then she would have to cross the other steamer's stern which would lose valuable time. The *Jeanie* was fast and always up for a race and it is said that she managed to overhaul *Columba* when she was brand new with guests on board although MacBrayne always complained that their vessel wasn't really trying! Whatever the ins and outs of it *Jeanie* was undeniably fast and the 1930s LM&SR paddlers were no match for her. However, she very rarely ever bested *Duchess of Montrose* so, honour was satisfied.

***King Edward* (1901) off Innellan 19th July 1930.** After being replaced on the long distance sailings from Princes Pier and Gourock by *King George V* in 1926 *King Edward* was transferred to All the Way sailings from Glasgow, thus greatly enhancing the Glasgow fleet. Her normal sailing was that at 1000 which took her to Dunoon, Rothesay, Largs, Millport (Keppel) and then on to various points on the Arran Coast on a non landing cruise. On the way down river calls were also made at Govan and Renfrew. At the latter train connections could be maintained to and from Paisley. Her transfer served as a boost to the Williamson-Buchanan fleet and boosted the traffic from Glasgow and from the individual resorts and her greater speed allowed her on most days to actually get quite close to the Arran coast rather than the somewhat distant view that her paddle predecessors had managed!

Mercury **(1892) passing off Innellan 15th July 1933.** When built, *Mercury* was a flyer, designed to overcome the vessels of the CSP on the basic services in and out of Rothesay and was capable of a speed of around 18 knots. For the early part of her life she was associated with the Kyles of Bute run and could happily take on all comers. Sadly, the years weren't kind to her and she slowed down appreciably. In LM&SR days she was downgraded to basic connectional work and normally worked in partnership with *Duchess of Fife*. Like all the former G&SWR vessels she was directly owned by the LM&SR and flew their houseflag. 1933 proved to be her final year in service as she was sold for scrap in December of that year. An interesting feature of this photograph is that she is flying the Pilot Exemption flag under the Red Ensign at the stern, a feature of the South Bank fleet for several years in the early 1930s.

Marchioness of Graham **passing Innellan 6th June 1936.** *Marchioness of Graham* was designed to operate on the Ardrossan to Arran service as consort to *Glen Sannox*, replacing *Atalanta*. She was used all year round on the service and was strongly built to cope with the tumultuous winter seas. At that time Ardrossan was used as the mainland port all year round but, as now, the vessel frequently had to divert to another port when Ardrossan was unusable. In summer the two vessel service only got started in mid June and this allowed the *Graham* to be used elsewhere. She was frequently based at Gourock and took the Arran via the Kyles sailing while the regular cruise vessels were engaged in charter or special sailings. Although she couldn't have been called a handsome vessel she was neat in the water and well designed for her designated role.

***Eagle III* passing Toward July 1928.** Carrying what looks like a good load *Eagle III* has just rounded Toward Point on her way to Rothesay from Glasgow. Just to the left of her mast just above the lifejacket locker can be discerned the top of Toward Point Lighthouse. Situated at the south end of the Cowal peninsula Toward was the point which all steamers heading to and from Rothesay had to round and in inclement weather it could prove to be a lively spot which caught many a traveller unawares. Situated just to the north of the lighthouse on the Dunoon side lay Toward Pier which was reckoned to be one of the most difficult piers on the Clyde to use. Surrounded by rocks there was literally only one course in and out which, if deviated from, could prove to be disastrous. Thus, the Wemyss Bay steamer *Lady Gertrude* was wrecked there in the 1870s. Such was its complexity it had largely been abandoned as a calling point by the early 1920s.

***Minard* (1926) off Toward Point 17th July 1937.** On what looks like an excellent day with a sea like glass *Minard* can be seen on her way to Glasgow, most likely inbound from the Loch Fyne ports. These included Inveraray, Crarae, Ardrishaig, Tarbert where she berthed in the Inner Harbour, Otter Ferry and Skipness. The last two points were visited usually once per week on what would have been their only calls by a steamer. In 1937 Clyde Cargo Steamers was amalgamated with the Campbeltown Company to form the Clyde and Campbeltown Shipping Co. This organisation was owned by MacBraynes and, in that year, all the vessels received red and black funnels which, in *Minard*'s case, added some welcome colour to her appearance. Compared to one of their vessels on an outward journey her decks are not cluttered with cargo but more than likely she would have been carrying livestock heading for the markets in Greenock and Glasgow.

Atalanta (1906) alongside Wemyss Bay 4th August 1930. This rare photograph depicts the turbine steamer *Atalanta* lying at the Millport Berth at Wemyss Bay. For some reason for a period in 1930 the LM&SR decided to switch *Atalanta* to the Fairlie to Millport service while *Glen Rosa* became the secondary Arran steamer in her stead. By this time the Fairlie steamer's roster included a call at Wemyss Bay. Behind her can be seen the magnificent station at Wemyss Bay. A covered walkway took passengers from the pier up to the station which was at a higher level. This building each summer was festooned in a lovely selection of floral displays which delighted train and steamer passengers. The berth at the other side of the pier was the Rothesay Berth and it was the case that never the twain should be mixed up. If nothing else, this usually prevented passengers getting on board the wrong steamer! The large building on the hill is Kelly House.

Mercury (1892 and *Glen Rosa* (1893) departing Wemyss Bay 9th August 1930. This was a scene repeated several times a day at Wemyss Bay. The connecting train from Glasgow has disgorged a large number of passengers bound for Rothesay and Millport. Those for the former destination would have been guided to *Mercury* while Millport passengers would have gone to *Glen Rosa*. Both vessels would each have reversed out of the pier. In this instance *Glen Rosa* has left first and has reversed quite a distance before turning to starboard to head for Largs. *Mercury*, meanwhile has reversed only a short distance and is quickly crossing *Glen Rosa*'s wake before turning hard to starboard for Rothesay. *Glen Rosa* would then cross *Mercury*'s wake to gain her course. This was an exciting manoeuvre to watch and it depended on smart movement on the part of the respective skippers to keep to a tight timetable while avoiding each other.

***Minard* (1925) and *Ardyne* (1928) off Craigmore 14th May 1932.** To many people the vessels of Clyde Cargo Steamers were virtually invisible yet they were some of the most important craft to ply their trade on the Firth. They carried the various cargoes scorned by the more famous paddlers and turbines without which the small towns and villages could not have survived. Every day apart from the Sabbath several of their vessels would sail from Glasgow's Kingston Dock around 0400 to various parts of the firth including the Cowal piers, the Bute piers, Cumbrae and Arran. In addition there was a thrice weekly sailing all the way to Inveraray at the head of Loch Fyne. In this unusual shot *Minard* on the left is coming from Loch Fyne en route to Glasgow while *Ardyne* is heading for Rothesay. They had probably the most uninspiring colour scheme of all being black all over with a red underbody. In the background are Canada Hill and Craigmore on Bute.

***Juno* (1898) berthing at Craigmore July 1929.** This evocative photograph taken from another vessel shows the Ayr excursion vessel *Juno* in the act of coming alongside at Craigmore. Having slowed right down she has passed close to the pier to enable fore and aft heaving lines to be thrown on to the pier where they would be quickly grabbed by pier staff and the mooring ropes put over bollards. Once fixed the vessel would start to go astern while the lines were winched in to bring the vessel alongside the pier and a gangway would be quickly run aboard to allow disembarkation to commence. This would be a quick affair with the passenger "encouraged" to move quickly! Most of the small piers were rather basic affairs but Craigmore possessed an impressive shore building including an archway which can be seen just above the aft lifeboat. There passengers would be met with a pier official demanding the payment of pier dues.

Mercury* (1892) pulls away from Craigmore Pier.** Photographed from another vessel we can see ***Mercury coming out of Craigmore on the short journey to Rothesay. Craigmore was an interesting pier in that it was one of the small number of piers that were of iron construction whereas the normal one-berth pier on the Clyde was normally of wooden construction. However, in Craigmore's case, the walkway on to the pier was of an ornate metal construction as can be seen in this photograph. The actual pier head alongside which the vessel berthed however was of wooden construction, this being decidedly better for the inevitable slamming alongside of a vessel. Craigmore was also blessed with a very ornate pier building; between the funnel and the navigating bridge can be seen the shore arch under which passengers exited and entered the pier. This had a waiting room on one side and accommodation for the pier master on the other and still survives to this day.

Duchess of Argyll* (1906) approaching Craigmore 19th July 1930.** The crack Caledonian turbine steamer ***Duchess of Argyll is captured approaching Craigmore on a summer's day carrying a good complement of passengers. With the success of the world's first commercially operated turbine steamer ***King Edward*** introduced in 1901 and her consort ***Queen Alexandra*** which was delivered the following year the Caley Company realised they had to respond in kind by having such a vessel themselves. Thus, ***Duchess of Argyll*** was built in 1906 and introduced on to the Ardrossan to Arran service in competition to the G&SW's flyer ***Glen Sannox***. Very quickly the Caledonian Steam Packet were rewarded for their initiative when their vessel consistently beat the older paddler in their daily races and greatly improved the Company's profile and share of the traffic. The Caley turbine became a well-loved steamer on the Clyde and continued in service until 1951. Even then she wasn't finished and began a new career as a floating laboratory at Portland, lasting as such until 1970.

Duchess of Argyll **(1906) leaving Craigmore.** After the Great War ***Duchess of Argyll*** became identified with the Arran via the Kyles cruise from Princes Pier, Gourock and Wemyss Bay through the Kyles to the Arran ports of Corrie, Brodick, Lamlash and Whiting Bay thereafter returning up Firth via the Sound of Bute along the east coast of Bute. On the way she called at Dunoon, Craigmore and Tighnabruaich and this picture shows her leaving Craigmore on the outward journey. Given the proximity of Rothesay it might seem strange that she stopped at Craigmore but it was the "fashionable" end of the town and was popular as a base for upper middle class holidaymakers. She became completely synonymous with this route until 1936 when she was transferred to the Campbeltown and Inveraray routes which the CSP inherited with their takeover of Williamson-Buchanan and Turbine Steamers.

***Atalanta* (1906) gliding across Rothesay Bay.** Having already called at Rothesay *Atalanta* can be seen here slowing down in order to call at Craigmore. The actual sailing time between the two points was barely five minutes which meant that for the seamen it made sense to stay in their berthing positions rather than move away. *Atalanta* was a vessel not renowned for speed but she had one distinction probably not appreciated by her passengers, that of being somewhat lively in a rough sea. While any vessel would be affected by such conditions, she seemed particularly unfortunate and it was often said that she would have been capable of rolling while in drydock! As she spent much of her time sailing in the outer firth and Clyde summers could often produce stormy seas many of her passengers must have really suffered the agonies! That being said, *Atalanta* did what was asked of her by her owners throughout her career and was quickly snapped up by new owners when she was withdrawn from Clyde service.

***Duchess of Fife* (1903) approaching Craigmore 9th August 1930.** Reckoned by many people to be the prettiest paddle steamer ever built for Clyde service *Duchess of Fife* was introduced into Clyde service by the CSP in 1903. She was designed to serve on the "bread and butter" services to Dunoon, Rothesay and the Kyles from the railheads at Gourock and Wemyss Bay and was designed to be in use all year round. Such was the perfection of her hull design that her bow wake rose perfectly into the paddles. Although not designed to be a racer her four cylinder triple expansion two-crank machinery managed a creditable 17.55 knots during her trials. Although her daily work was not as glamorous as the cruising and tourist steamers it was the backbone of her owner's services and earned a substantial amount of revenue. She continued on such services during the 1920s and 30s and right up to the end of her life she was still used for around 10 months of the year.

Duchess of Fife **(1903) leaving Craigmore on 19th July 1930.** Having briefly called at Craigmore ***Duchess of Fife*** is slowly gaining speed on a railway connectional sailing to probably Wemyss Bay. The rosters of the railway connectional vessels were rather complicated with the ***Fife*** and her consort, until 1933 ***Mercury*** and thereafter ***Duchess of Rothesay*** and then ***Queen-Empress***, changing on a daily basis. Thus, the first would berth overnight at Rothesay and make for Gourock via the Cowal piers, following this with a cargo sailing to Dunoon before returning down the firth to Rothesay. After serving Wemyss Bay she would end her day at Auchenlochan. Next day she would start there and spend the morning sailing to Wemyss Bay before heading for Gourock in the early afternoon. Thereafter she returned to Rothesay and spent the rest of the day sailing to Wemyss Bay before overnighting at Rothesay and starting the whole process again. The concept of sailing from A to B was totally unknown until the 1950s.

Glen Sannox **(1925) and** ***Kenilworth*** **(1898) off Craigmore 4th June 1932.** Even although it was a suburb of Rothesay, Craigmore enjoyed a remarkable number of steamer calls on any one day, so many in fact that it was known as the "Charing Cross of the Clyde". Virtually every vessel, with the exception of some of the tourist and cruise vessels, called while sailing to and from Rothesay and this made it a great position for taking photographs of the steamers. In this shot the LM&SR turbine ***Glen Sannox*** is leaving while the L&NER's ***Kenilworth*** is approaching. As the name would suggest the former was built for the Arran service but was used elsewhere, particularly early in the Summer timetable. ***Kenilworth*** was a railway connectional vessel sailing out of Craigendoran on the basic sailings to Dunoon and Rothesay and served her owners faithfully for 40 years before being withdrawn in 1938.

Marchioness of Breadalbane **(1890) leaving Craigmore 16th July 1932.** In 1890 the one year old Caledonian Steam Packet Company took over the running of the services from the CR terminal at Wemyss Bay in the place of a private contractor and ordered two new vessels to provide them, one of which was the ***Breadalbane***. In her early years she found herself employed on the various services from Gourock and Wemyss Bay but after the Great War she was principally used on the Millport service with a daily call at Kilchattan Bay on Bute. Thus, it would have been relatively unusual to find her calling at Craigmore. From 1933 she replaced her quasi sister ***Caledonia*** on the Holy Loch service, remaining as such until the delivery of ***Marchioness of Lorne*** in 1935. The ***Breadalbane*** was never a showy vessel and was never considered to be a "crack" steamer. However, she was a dependable one and her owners could have had no complaints during her 45 year Clyde career. Noticeable in this photograph are her original fan destination boards.

Columba **(1878) off Craigmore June 1929.** Probably the most famous steamer ever to sail on the Clyde was ***Columba*** sailing from Glasgow to Tarbert and Ardrishaig on the first leg of the Royal Route which followed part of the route taken by Queen Victoria in a visit in 1847. Her time of departure from Glasgow for most of her life was 0711 and it was claimed that anyone in the city anywhere near the river could set their watches by her progress down the river. She never digressed from the route for which she was built and was only in service for four months per year. In 1928 MacBrayne was taken over by a combination of Coast Lines and the London, Midland and Scottish Railway and in 1929 someone decided that the fleet needed a new image which led to hulls being painted grey instead of black. Such was the outbreak of fury on Clydeside at what was seen as vandalism ***Columba***'s hull was repainted black in a matter of weeks. Clydesiders cared deeply about their steamers!

Marchioness of Breadalbane **(1890) sailing toward Rothesay August 1929.** In 1890 the CSP took over the steamer services out of Wemyss Bay to Rothesay and Millport and had two vessels constructed for the routes. The first of these, with the longest service in the fleet, was ***Marchioness of Breadalbane***. A typical vessel of her period, the ***Breadalbane*** spent almost her entire life sailing out of Wemyss Bay, mostly on the service to Millport. This involved calls at Largs, Millport (Keppel), Millport (Old) and Kilchattan Bay. However, it also involved a call at Rothesay on Saturdays when her capacity was required to help cope with the numbers travelling to Bute. She lasted in all year round service until early 1935 but, from late 1933, she acted as a replacement for ***Caledonia*** on the Holy Loch service and kept the berth warm until the appearance on ***Marchioness of Lorne*** in 1935. In the background is ***Duchess of Argyll*** leaving the Bay.

Isle of Arran **(1892) approaching Rothesay June 1931.** Having been built by Buchanan to operate on the Broomielaw-Arran service this popular vessel soon settled down to operating from Glasgow to Rothesay with cruises to the Arran Coast or the Kyles of Bute. Despite the rigours of sailing down a river that at times approximated to an open sewer the sailings from Glasgow maintained their popularity with particularly working class Glaswegians. By the inter war years the river had been cleaned up and the Williamson Buchanan fleet made a good living from the Glasgow business. With the addition of ***King Edward*** to the Glasgow fleet in 1927 ***Isle of Arran*** was relegated to a variety of duties that in June included standing in for the turbine when she was on charter business. After a lifetime of good service the arrival of ***Queen Mary*** in 1933 rendered her unemployed and she was sold off the river. In the background can be seen ***Waverley*** taking her ease at a buoy in the bay.

Bute 4 **in Rothesay Bay in July 1931.** This vessel was originally built for Hill & Company in 1898 and employed by them in the upper firth. Hill was one of the companies that were joined together to form Clyde Cargo Steamers and the vessel was transferred to their ownership. She was blessed with rather a large funnel which made her stand out in the fleet and she had the distinction of being the only vessel employed on Clyde service that carried an Arabic numeral in her name. In this photograph she is emitting a prodigious amount of black smoke which would not endear her to the locals and is carrying cargo piled up on both the main deck and on the top deck. She had a successful career and served her owners well until she was withdrawn in 1935.

Eagle III **(1910) approaching Rothesay 4th June 1932.** *Eagle III* is seen arriving at Rothesay packed to the gunwales with passengers on what looks like an excellent day. Although many passengers from the Glasgow area travelled to the coast resorts by means of trains to the railheads and then by steamer on the relatively short sea journey, many still preferred the idea of sailing all the way from the city down the Clyde and in to the firth. One of the undoubted attractions of such a journey was sailing past the busy wharves and shipyards of the Clyde in Glasgow. Unlike now, the Clyde was alive with shipping of all shapes and sizes bringing in and taking out copious amounts of cargo of all kinds. Another attraction was the fact that the vessels called at the piers at Govan and Renfrew on the way down which made travel easy for the residents of each. Williamson Buchanan were adept at marketing and a popular ploy was offering an all-in ticket for travel which also included lunch and/or high tea.

***King George V* off Craigmore 4th June 1932.** *King George V* was a revolutionary vessel, Parsons' answer to the marine diesel engine. With Yarrow boilers and high pressure machinery she was planned to have comparable running costs to the diesel engine. Sadly, the experiment was not successful and the vessel gave her owners a torrid time in her early years. After two years, her boilers were removed and replaced with Babcock and Wilcox boilers which in turn were replaced by a conventional navy boiler working at normal pressure, in 1935. During the 1928 reboilering her funnels were fitted with cowls and it is this condition that she appears in this photograph. To her left can be seen the bow of an ocean going vessel. During the Depression years many such vessels found themselves without employment and were laid up in such places as Rothesay Bay, the Kyles of Bute, the Holy Loch and the Gareloch. Note the lifeboat dangling over the side; presumably it was used to fetch supplies for the anchor watch on board.

***Marmion* (1906) arriving in Rothesay Bay 4th June 1932.** Here we can see the L&NER's *Marmion* steaming towards Rothesay blowing her whistle to presumably warn other craft to get out of her way as she lines up to take the pier. This shot demonstrates the traditional North Bank colour scheme of black hull with gold lines, cream coloured upperworks, stained deck shelters and a red, white and black funnel. While the LM&SR chose to merge the former CR and G&SWR vessels into a new colour scheme the L&NER perpetuated the colour scheme inherited from the NBR. In some quarters this colour scheme was felt to be very dull and conservative for the 1930s. She is dressed overall which usually indicated that a vessel was under charter to a private organisation. Such charters were a lucrative source of additional income to shipping companies in the early and late season and could take vessels to piers which they would normally have never called at in ordinary service. The companies were frequently prepared to trim their normal timetables in order to fit in such sailings.

Jupiter **(1896) off Craigmore 17th July 1932.** One of the undoubted crack steamers built for the G&SWR in the late 1890s was *Jupiter*, a product of Clydebank and introduced in 1896. Largely employed on the Arran via the Kyles service, she could show a clean pair of heels to her Caley and NBR contemporaries. However, time was not kind to her and by the 1930s she was a veritable slowcoach and was employed on rosters where speed was not a consideration. In this shot she is on the Afternoon Cruise roster which included a lunchtime sailing from Rothesay direct to Millport. As the photograph shows this was not exactly a sailing which was tremendously well-used! At her masthead she is flying the LM&S houseflag which consisted of a red square with a white cross; with the Grouping of 1923 the former G&SW ships were transferred to LM&S ownership because of legal restrictions upon their use while the former Caley vessels remained in CSP ownership. As the 1930s progressed such vessels were withdrawn while their replacements were owned from the outset by the CSP. By 1937 only two vessels remained in LM&S ownership and they were then transferred to the CSP.

Isle of Arran **(1892) off Craigmore 17th July 1932.** Throughout her life *Isle of Arran* was one of the vessels that each day sailed down the River Clyde from the heart of Glasgow bound for the various resorts on the Firth of Clyde thus perpetuating a service begun with *Comet* in 1812. She was originally owned by Buchanan Steamers and carried the somewhat bland funnel colouring of black with a white stripe. However, in 1919, her owners and John Williamson combined to form the Williamson-Buchanan fleet and the latter's funnel colouring of white with black top was adopted for the whole fleet although the ring on the funnels of the former Buchanan vessels could still be seen. *Isle of Arran* led a highly successful career of sailing from Glasgow before being withdrawn in 1933 to make way for the new turbine steamer *Queen Mary* which was introduced that year. She was immediately sold to Thames interests and quickly left the Clyde to begin a new life sailing out of London. This lasted for three years until she was finally withdrawn and broken up in 1936.

King George V **passing Craigmore 6th August 1932.** *King George* is heading into Rothesay on her daily sailing to Inveraray. Starting at Princes Pier at 0850 she called at Gourock at 0913, Dunoon at 0930 and Rothesay at 1010 before continuing on into the Kyles of Bute to call at Tighnabruaich and then heading for Loch Fyne and a call at Crarae before arriving at Inveraray at 1310. Passengers were allowed an hour to explore the delights of the planned Highland village before returning by the same route. However, passengers could leave her at Inveraray and join a coach which took them to Dunoon via the shores of Loch Eck. Once at Dunoon they had time to wander round before rejoining *King George* for the journey back to their starting point. In the days of *Lord of the Isles* the Loch Eck Tour included sailing on the loch by steamer but after the Great War a more prosaic motor coach was used.

Duchess of Hamilton **(1932) passing Craigmore 18th September 1932.** After the outstanding success of *Duchess of Montrose* introduced in 1930 the LM&SR management were only too happy to order a sister ship for delivery in 1932. She was almost a copy of the original vessel but did incorporate some differences, the most obvious of which was the provision of a full length mainmast. She was designed to replace the former G&SWR *Juno* on the excursions out of Ayr, Troon and Ardrossan and, after some hesitation on the part of regular passengers, became very successful. The Ayr season ended in early September but the management decided to keep the *Hamilton* in service for the rest of the month in 1932 on the *Montrose*'s cruises from Gourock while the latter was laid up early in Greenock. On this particular day she was bound for a cruise to Skate Island which also included a cruise round Bute. Note the laid up ships anchored in the bay, victims of the gathering Depression.

Jupiter (1896) approaching Rothesay 15th July 1933. The LM&SR stalwart *Jupiter* is pictured here making her approach to Rothesay carrying a goodly sized crowd. By this time the old vessel was employed on the Princes Pier to Ayr service and the Afternoon Cruise roster. On Saturdays this included the ever popular afternoon cruise to the Kyles of Bute which included calls at Colintraive, Tighnabruaich, Auchenlochan and at Ormidale and it is on this sailing that she is employed here. Most of her passengers would disembark to enjoy the delights of the Bute resort but a reasonable number would have remained on board for the Kyles cruise. In her youth, *Jupiter* was employed on the Arran via the Kyles cruise but by the 1930s calls at Arran were for her rare. However, on the port after sponson, she still carries the steps required for disembarkation to the tender at Corrie, and at the bow can be seen the primitive canvas protection for the forward deck hand. Later steamers had a spurket plate for this purpose.

Duchess of Fife (1903) and *Waverley* (1899) in Rothesay Bay 15th July 1933. A very busy *Duchess of Fife* is caught here sailing toward the pier at Rothesay with a large crowd of passengers on board. Throughout her long life the *Fife* served on the railway connection sailings to and from the Coast resorts maintaining the basic services that the towns depended on and which were the main earners for the railway companies. Up until 1937 her duties took her from Gourock and Wemyss Bay to Dunoon, Rothesay and the Kyles of Bute and in this instance she is arriving at the resort from Wemyss Bay. In the background can be seen the L&NER's *Waverley* which is manoeuvring at a mooring buoy in the bay. Such was the demand for berths at Rothesay that any vessel which had a gap in her roster left the pier and moored at buoys until it was time to return to load passengers. These buoys were also on occasion used as overnight berths, no doubt to the chagrin of the crews who were denied time in Rothesay's night spots!

Duchess of Montrose* (1930) arriving at Rothesay 15th July 1933.** This photograph shows the ***Montrose in her original condition. Having a mainmast which was only half the length of the foremast was a blemish on the appearance of the otherwise sleek cruising turbine and gave her an unbalanced profile. She made her name by providing a series of cruises around the Firth and on this particular day she is bound on an excursion around Arran and Ailsa Craig. Her routing was slightly strange in that after the Rothesay call she then crossed to Wemyss Bay to make another train connection but this also included a connection from Edinburgh (Princes Street). Even before her Rothesay call she is well loaded and by the time she had called at Rothesay, Wemyss Bay, Largs and Millport (Keppel) her passenger total would have been very near her complement leading to a very busy day for the Purser and the catering department.

Marmion* (1906) in Rothesay Bay with the Cowal Hills behind 15th July 1933.** One of the most pleasing aspects of Clyde Steamer history has been the systems used by the various companies for naming vessels. Thus the CR fleet mostly adopted the system of naming vessels after noble ladies while the G&SWR named their vessels after Roman deities, the only exception being that vessels for Arran were named after Arran glens. The NBR used characters from the works of Walter Scott as their inspiration for names, such as ***Marmion. While this may suggest a literary input into their affairs it actually grew out of the roots of the company which were in the Border lands associated with Scott. Another delight has been the fact that individual names were perpetuated in successive generations of vessels. With the appearance of ***Talisman*** in 1935 ***Marmion*** was downgraded to the basic services to Rothesay and had her winter appearances cut back.

King George V* (1926) at speed in Rothesay Bay 15th July 1933.** Carrying an immense number of passengers, ***King George V is powering across Rothesay Bay on the outward leg of her weekday journey from Greenock (Princes Pier) and Gourock to Inveraray. After making a brief call at the pier she continued on to Tighnabruaich and Loch Fyne. She is shown in her 1929 condition when she was reboilered and fitted with cowls on her funnels. The whole concept of the vessel was a brave experiment in producing a high powered turbine steamer that was capable of providing competition to the diesel engine which sadly never achieved real success. She is shown with all her flags at half-mast in memory of Hugh McFarlane, the recently deceased Managing Director of Williamson-Buchanan Steamers.

Queen Mary* (1933) arriving at Rothesay 15th July 1933. *Queen Mary was the new vessel of 1933 and was the "pin up steamer" of the Williamson-Buchanan fleet. This large and commodious vessel brought new standards of comfort and quality to the Bridge Wharf fleet and became an instant hit with the Glasgow public. She was normally employed on the 1000 sailing from Bridge Wharf and gave Rothesay bound passengers over four hours ashore in the Bute capital. While they enjoyed themselves exploring the various delights Rothesay had to offer the vessel continued on to Largs, Keppel and then gave a cruise to the Arran Coast which brought a new crowd of customers on board. On a particularly busy day her passenger figures combining each portion of the journey could easily top 4,000 souls which gave her an impressive end of season total.

Jeanie Deans **(1931) off Craigmore 16th July 1933.** From 1932 ***Jeanie Deans***, flagship of the L&NER's Clyde fleet, was employed on a series of special cruises which were organised to compete with those of ***Duchess of Montrose***. These also included special Sunday excursions from Craigendoran which took her to all corners of the Firth, many of which had not seen the red, white and black funnels for years if at all. One such place was the destination on this Sunday – Lady Isle off Troon. On her way there and back her route took her Round Cumbrae. As well as being a very busy pier Craigmore was also an excellent place to view steamers in general as all inbound vessels to Rothesay from the east and south passed very close on the way in to Rothesay Bay thus affording enthusiasts many photographic opportunities. Seen to advantage in this photograph are the fore saloon and extended funnels added to the steamer in 1932.

Queen Mary **(1933) sailing into Rothesay 16th July 1933.** On another day during the high season ***Queen Mary*** arrives at Rothesay on her way to the Arran Coast. Although the bulk of her passengers would disembark at Rothesay some did stay on for the afternoon cruise and they would be joined by afternoon excursionists at Largs and Millport Keppel. In pre-war days the phrase "Arran Coast" actually contained different destinations each day of the week, Thus, in 1936, on Mondays she went to Brodick and Corrie, on Tuesdays to Lochranza, Wednesdays to Lamlash, Thursdays to Skipness and Fridays to Round Inchmarnock. All were non-landing and how close she got depended on whether she was running late! A popular feature on board was that a passenger could buy a combined cruise ticket and lunch and high tea for one price. In 1936 this would have cost 8/6d for Saloon passengers.

Duchess of Argyll (1906) at speed in Rothesay Bay 14th July 1934. With her decks crowded with passengers the pioneer Caley turbine heads to Rothesay on her morning call. From the end of the Great War until the end of the 1935 season the ***Argyll*** was employed on the Arran via the Kyles sailing which took her from Princes Pier and Gourock via the Kyles to the East Arran ports of Corrie, Brodick, Lamlash and Whiting Bay. Time ashore was given at each port and she returned by way of the Main Channel. At Corrie, her passengers used a ferry to get to and from the shore, the only such ferry used by the LM&SR fleet. She was reckoned to be at the peak of her performance at this juncture and for many years she was commanded by the legendary John McNaughton who was reckoned by many to be one of the finest Clyde masters. Although by this stage her facilities had been outclassed by the ***Duchess of Montrose*** and ***Duchess of Hamilton***, she was still held in great affection by the travelling public.

Duchess of Montrose (1930) arriving at Rothesay 14th July 1934. When built, ***Duchess of Montrose*** was given a half-sized mainmast but this was replaced in 1934 with a full size version which greatly enhanced her appearance. She was regarded as the premier cruise vessel in the LM&SR fleet and operated to various points throughout the Firth. This photograph is relatively unusual in that it is taken on a Saturday, the one day that her cruise did not include a call at Rothesay. However, the day is Glasgow Fair Saturday and she is employed in the forenoon on relief runs between Wemyss Bay and Rothesay. She has probably followed the regular vessel across taking the passengers that had been left at Wemyss Bay. For her passengers this would have been an unexpected bonus, particularly for those with Steerage tickets! Not often would they have been allowed to travel on a First Class steamer without being asked to pay for a supplementary ticket.

Caledonia (1934) leaving Rothesay 14th July 1934. In her first season *Caledonia* was placed on the Afternoon Cruise roster. On weekdays, this took her away from Princes Pier at 0925 bound for Rothesay with calls at Gourock and Wemyss Bay. Once there, from Mondays to Fridays, she lay in until lunchtime before heading to Millport to begin her cruise. However, on Saturdays, she was rostered to return empty to Gourock to give a quick round trip to Dunoon before proceeding to Princes Pier to take the afternoon cruise to the Kyles of Bute piers, including Ormidale in Loch Riddon. This photograph captures her on the way back to Gourock after her first down run of the day. Free from the impediment of carrying passengers most of the crew were able to take a breather and enjoy the weather if it was clement and we can see some of them taking their ease on deck. Once back upriver it would have been to normal duties for all of them. Few of the passengers realised that the crews invariably worked up to 16 hours a day with little time off during the season to keep the services running.

Marmion (1906) approaches Rothesay with *Eagle III* (1910) in the background 31st August 1934. *Marmion* was one of the typical Clyde workhorses that maintained the basic services from the railheads to the Coast while never being regarded as part of the Premier League of vessels. In her case she was used all the year round on the service to the Holy Loch, Dunoon and Rothesay. During the main season she was principally employed on the Kyles of Bute service which involved a morning sailing to Rothesay followed by an afternoon cruise to Tighnabruaich and Auchenlochan with time ashore. Lying in the bay is Williamson Buchanan's *Eagle III* which is taking her ease before performing the early afternoon sailing back to Glasgow (Bridge Wharf). Such were the number of calls at Rothesay's pier that at times it was impossible for a vessel with time in hand to spend it lying at the pier. Instead, they moved out into the bay and lay at a buoy until it was time to return to the pier to load for the next sailing.

***Ardyne* (1928) arriving at Rothesay 1st June 1935.** The vessels of Clyde Cargo Steamers were some of the most important but least appreciated vessels in Clyde service. While they were distinctly lacking in the romance of the passenger vessels they were vital to the continued existence of the various towns and hamlets as they were responsible for bringing in many of the lifeline supplies that each calling point depended on. While the railway steamers happily carried parcels and livestock they were not equipped to convey the heavier bulk cargoes which were the prerogative of the cargo vessels. As each vessel was equipped with its own cargo handling gear they were able to use the same piers as the passenger vessels and with their dull colour scheme of black with red boot topping they provided a distinct contrast to the brighter painted larger vessels. The cargo vessels survived into the postwar world but found it hard to compete with the improving road services and then the car ferries and all had disappeared by the late 1950s.

Atalanta* (1906) sailing into Rothesay Bay 1st June 1935.** Although normally employed as the second vessel on the Arran service each summer her timetable normally only began in the middle of June. This allowed her to be utilised before this on whatever route she was required on. One market that the LM&SR were particularly focussed on developing was that of chartering vessels out to a variety of organisations to undertake a sailing of their choice. This meant that frequently the cruising turbines and the 1934 paddlers ***Caledonia and ***Mercury*** were unavailable to operate their normal sailings and other vessels such as ***Atalanta*** were called in to replace them. Whatever roster ***Atalanta*** was operating on here was not exactly well supported as only one passenger can be seen about her decks! Photographs taken at the beginning of summer usually showed vessels with paintwork in pristine condition with waterlines intact and no rust marks but, as the season wore on, the paintwork become somewhat shabbier. Such was the intensity of the rosters worked very little time was available for touching up the paintwork.

***Queen Alexandra* (1912) approaching Rothesay 13th July 1935.** An exceedingly smoky *Queen Alexandra* powers her way into Rothesay on a lovely summer day. She is, to put it mildly, heavily loaded and there appears to be virtually no open deck space left! The fact that she is well loaded can also be testified to by the fact that her waterline is barely discernible. This particular day was Glasgow Fair Saturday which meant that she was specially employed on the Inveraray service so that she could also carry MacBrayne traffic. On Fair Saturday the Inveraray sailing diverted via Tarbert and Ardrishaig to act as an overflow for *Columba*, such was the traffic heading for the Loch Fyne ports, Gigha and Islay. This resulted in her arrival at Inveraray being delayed as was the return sailing to Gourock and Princes Pier. She would have been significantly quieter on the return journey. Most on board would be unaware that this was the last season they could do this excursion on a Williamson vessel and that 1936 would introduce a totally different world on the Clyde.

***Saint Columba* (1912) crosses Rothesay Bay 29th August 1936.** In 1935 MacBrayne retired the veterans *Columba* and *Iona* and replaced them with *Queen Alexandra* and *King George V*. The sale was completed in October 1935 and the two vessels immediately had their funnels repainted red. Such was the fame of *Columba* that MacBrayne had the problem of replacing her with *Queen Alexandra* in a way that would be acceptable to the public and their final plan was brilliant. She was given the name *Saint Columba* so as not to appear a second rate copy of the venerable institution and was modernised. Thus, her top deck was extended and under the extension was built the Clachan Bar modelled on a West Highland hostelry. Her original funnels were replaced with more modern, thicker versions and she was given a third thus making her both eye catching and unique on the Clyde. She also became the only Clyde steamer to have onboard signs repeated in German to reflect where some of her traffic came from! A comparison between this image and the previous one illustrates well the changes that took place in the same steamer's appearance.

Queen-Empress (1912) arriving at Rothesay on 18th August 1935. *Queen-Empress* was very much the maid of all work in the Williamson-Buchanan fleet and could be found undertaking a variety of jobs. This particular day was a Sunday and she took a sailing at 1000 from Bridge Wharf to Dunoon and Rothesay only with just over 400 passengers from the city. This sailing acted as a relief to *Queen Mary II* at 1030 and *King Edward* at 1100 to avoid them "boiling over". After unloading she would have vacated the pier to await departure time and would have moved to the steamer moorings in the bay. Lying there already is *Marmion* of the L&NER fleet. These moorings were a feature of Rothesay Bay right up until the 1950s but, in the 1930s, it was not uncommon to see four or five vessels lying there leaving the pier available for other vessels.

Duchess of Argyll (1906) passing off Craigmore 6th June 1936. In 1935 the LM&SR/CSP fleet was boosted by the taking over of the Williamson-Buchanan fleet in early October. From 1936 they became responsible for the Inveraray and Campbeltown services previously operated by Turbine Steamers. Both services became the responsibility of *Duchess of Argyll* which now operated to Inveraray on Mondays, Wednesdays and Fridays and to Lochranza and Campbeltown on Tuesdays, Thursdays and Saturdays. This photo, taken on Saturday 6th June, shows her passing lightly loaded on the outward sailing to Kintyre after calling at Rothesay on route to Fairlie then Lochranza. In an effort to provide passengers with some extra shelter on the promenade and top decks canvas dodgers were fitted in certain places, not exactly the most effective way of breaking the sea breezes!

Mercury* (1934) arriving at Rothesay 6th June 1936.** When the LM&SR came into being in 1923 it absorbed both the G&SWR and the CR fleets. The former vessels were restricted on where they could sail and so were registered in the LM&SR's name while the latter, which were not restricted, remained in the name of the CR's subsidiary the CSP, which led to the anomalous situation of the fleet having two house flags. As new vessels were introduced in the 1930s some, including ***Mercury, were registered as LM&SR owned and, in this shot, it can be clearly seen that she is flying the LM&SR flag. As the fleet replacement continued in the 1930s most of the new vessels were CSP owned and, by 1937, only ***Mercury*** and ***Glen Rosa*** remained as LM&SR ships. Thus, in 1937, they were re-registered as CSP vessels and commenced flying the famous "yellow pennant" of that company.

Caledonia* (1934) sailing across Rothesay Bay 25th July 1936.** As well as causing a stir among enthusiasts and regular Coast travellers the 1934 paddlers also caused a commotion among steamer crews. Many felt that they were difficult to handle compared to their predecessors and they seemed incapable of running in a perfect straight line. This was put down to their large superstructure which at times acted like a sail and took them slightly off course. As a result alterations were carried out to both vessels to make them easier to handle. In ***Caledonia's case this involved the removal of the seven paddle floats on each wheel and their replacement with eight new floats. This alteration did serve to improve her performance but it came at the cost of a reduction in speed. In ***Mercury***'s case she went through two masters in her first season before she settled down under the steady hand of Captain Archie Campbell. Whatever deficiencies the new vessels had they made up for it in their usefulness and their ability to carry 1,900 passengers was a great asset at busy periods.

Duchess of Rothesay* (1895) arriving at Rothesay 15th August 1936.** This broadside shot clearly demonstrates just what an attractive looking vessel ***Duchess of Rothesay was and is a shining example of a later Victorian paddle steamer. The arrival of ***Caledonia*** and ***Mercury*** in 1934 had relegated ***Duchess of Rothesay*** temporarily from the Forenoon Kyles sailing and on to the basic sailings from Gourock and Wemyss Bay where she partnered her wee sister ***Duchess of Fife***. These rosters were very intensive leading to a very long working day for the crews who would start about 0500 on weekdays and not finish until around 2100. The early steamers were not renowned for the comfort of their crew accommodation and this was particularly true of the Rothesay where the seamen and firemen were accommodated in a very small compartment on the forward end of the lower deck. Despite the discomfort, many of her crew returned to her year after year and she was renowned as a happy ship.

Marmion* (1906) approaching Rothesay 15th August 1936.** Now adorned in the new L&NER colour scheme introduced that year ***Marmion is seen sailing into Rothesay pier. Throughout her career ***Marmion***'s appearance was changed on several occasions. When built, she had a large foresaloon on the main deck forward but during the Great War the promenade deck was extended right to the bow, as it was on her fleetmate ***Waverley***. While the Navy seemed to be happy with the transformation it was found on her return to civilian service that it hampered her performance and she was laid up after only one season. The built up bow was removed in 1923 and she was left with just a small foresaloon as pictured. She was then laid up again and, remarkably, it was 1926 before she finally returned to normal service. Thereafter she was an important unit in the fleet and normally saw service for ten months of the year until the appearance of the new ***Talisman*** in 1935.

Caledonia **(1934) approaching Rothesay 29th August 1936.** The phrase "the shock of the new" is a very apt description of the reception *Caledonia* received on entering service in 1934. With her sturdy build, deck saloons with an open deck above and a large funnel the vessel presented an entirely new profile to Clyde service. The main shock however was reserved for the design of her paddle boxes; from time immemorial Clyde paddlers had been built with well decorated and obvious paddle boxes but on *Caledonia* this custom was abandoned and in its place came disguised boxes with no vents or decoration but only imitation windows to allow for the escape of water. From a distance it wasn't obvious that the vessel was indeed a paddler and this was accentuated in a specially produced LM&SR publicity poster which portrayed her and her sister *Mercury* as if they had no paddles. To say their appearance caused a shock would be an understatement and many people took against them immediately which was unfortunate as both vessels were excellent additions to the Clyde fleet.

Waverley **(1899) approaching Rothesay 29th August 1936.** In this photograph the magnificent *Waverley* powers her way into Rothesay. Her main employment at this time was providing the sailing to Lochgoilhead and Arrochar as part of the famous Three Lochs Tour, the most important of the excursions provided by the L&NER on the Clyde. Upon her return to Craigendoran in the late afternoon she was utilised on a round trip to Rothesay which served to return cruise passengers to Dunoon and Rothesay and as a sailing for commuters returning to the Cowal ports and Rothesay. Her return sailing to Craigendoran provided the return connection for day trippers to the L&NER railway system. By 1936 the North Bank fleet played second fiddle to the LM&SR vessels and were rarely overwhelmed by the number of passengers using their services. Indeed, the only particularly busy period in the summer was the first fortnight in July which was the period of the Dumbarton and Clydebank Fair holidays when for obvious geographical reasons they sailed to the coast via Craigendoran. Such was the decline in numbers carried that a faction of L&NER shareholders were of the opinion that they should withdraw their vessels and instead contract the rival LM&SR fleet to connect into their trains.

King Edward (1901) approaching Rothesay 29th August 1936. With her decks completely packed with passengers the pioneer turbine glides towards the pier at Rothesay. 1936 was the first year that the Williamson Buchanan vessels were controlled by the LM&SR. To most passengers nothing would appear to have changed with the change of ownership but to the enthusiast of the day one change was very obvious in that all the ventilators were now painted silver as opposed to the old brown. As it was a Saturday, the vessel was employed on the 1000 sailing which was destined after Rothesay to call at Largs and Millport (Keppel) before cruising to the Arran Coast which on Saturdays meant the Fallen Rocks. Many of those on board would have disembarked at Rothesay but others would have joined her for the cruise to escape the hustle and bustle of a busy afternoon in the Bute resort.

Mercury (1934) paddles towards Rothesay pier with *Saint Columba* (1912) in the background heading for Ardrishaig via the Kyles. The appearance of the latter shows that it is mid morning and *Mercury* is arriving on a sailing from Greenock which included a call at Wemyss Bay at 1030. After an hour's rest she was away again at 1200 for Millport to begin her afternoon cruise from there to a variety of destinations. She replaced her sister *Caledonia* on this roster in 1936 while the latter took over the Arran via the Kyles service. In the late afternoon, on completion of the cruise, she sailed from Millport to Rothesay direct and finished with the important 1830 to Gourock and Greenock. As well as summer service, *Mercury* also saw service during the winter but this largely ceased on the appearance of *Jupiter* and *Juno* in 1937. Sadly, she was another vessel destined to be a war loss, a tragic end to a promising career.

***Arran* (1933) off Rothesay 10th July 1937.** This handy vessel was built in 1933 as a direct replacement to the previous vessel of the same name that had been wrecked on Barmore Island, Loch Fyne on 26th January of that year. As in the case of her predecessor she was usually to be found serving the ports of East Arran from Glasgow although she was also utilised on services to Dunoon and Rothesay. She was different from her fleetmates in that her engines and accommodation were aft as opposed to being amidships. In 1937 Clyde Cargo Steamers was amalgamated with the Campbeltown Co. to form Clyde & Campbeltown Shipping Co. under the ownership of MacBrayne. The vessels had their funnels repainted in MacBrayne red with black top and this was a decided improvement on the all black funnel of Clyde Cargo Steamers. Note the mounds of cargo piled up on her foredeck and on the top deck behind the bridge.

***Talisman* (1935) rumbles her way into Rothesay 10th July 1937.** *Talisman* is a vessel that to this day still causes arguments between enthusiasts. With her modern profile and noisy engines some felt that she was inferior to the graceful steam vessels of the past while others hailed her as a technical wonder. One point that all could agree on was that she was certainly different! Her profile was very much that of a modernised version of the classical Clyde passenger steamer though it was substantially ruined by the solid bulwarks on the forward promenade deck. The new L&NER colour scheme of 1936 also divided opinions with some thinking it absolutely ghastly while others saw it as a welcome relief from the sombre traditional colours of black and brown. However, one vessel that was improved by the new was *Talisman* as it nicely showed off her lines. Lying at the mooring in the bay is the L&NER flagship *Jeanie Deans*.

Jeanie Deans **(1931) leaving Rothesay 10th July 1937.** Introduced into service by the L&NER in 1931 *Jeanie Deans* made an instant impression on the Clyde trade. Initially, she was built with short funnels and a clear promenade deck toward the bow. However alterations were carried out which saw the funnels heightened by an unequal amount and a deck saloon constructed on the foredeck. Strangely, the windows in the latter were not of the same size which gave her an oddly unbalanced appearance. In an effort to revitalise their affairs a new colour scheme of grey hull with white upperworks was introduced in 1936 and it is in this colour scheme that the vessel is seen. On Saturdays in 1937 she was rostered to provide the 0843 connectional sailing to Rothesay and then returned to Craigendoran for an afternoon cruise Round Bute and it is on the morning sailing back to Craigendoran that she is employed in the picture, hence the apparent lack of any passengers.

Juno **(1937) leaving Rothesay Bay 10th July 1937.** The second of the 1937 twins, *Juno*, was delivered and entered service exactly one week before this photograph was taken. Several days earlier, on 6th July, invited guests were taken on her to the Kyles of Bute to show off the new vessel. The sisters were designed with year round service in mind and to this end were supplied with excellent covered accommodation. With there being only one dining saloon which was situated on the lower deck there was room for two saloons on the main deck and two deck shelters which was more than adequate for the sparse traffic normally carried during the winter months. As a result, both vessels proved popular with regular passengers. However, like the 1934 sisters, they could prove a handful for the crew in operation. *Juno* joined her sister on the basic services to Dunoon and Rothesay but was destined for a short life: sadly, she did not survive the Second World War. In September 1939 she was recorded as having called at Port Glasgow Steamboat Quay, a very rare occurrence in the 1930s. In the distance is *Caledonia* heading for the Kyles.

Minard **(1926) steams towards Rothesay 14th July 1934.** Given her somewhat unglamorous role *Minard* was quite a good looking vessel with her one mast and funnel being in perfect symmetry. The vessels of Clyde Cargo Steamers performed an essential role on the Clyde by carrying the important cargoes on which life depended in every settlement which the passenger vessels were not equipped to handle. Every single voyage would see their vessels filled with an amazing range of cargoes of anything from small items to large furniture containers by way of livestock. Households moving to and from the coast would send their belongings including furniture by their vessels in containers and it was one of these that contributed to the near loss of a predecessor, *Lapwing*, when it broke free while being unloaded at Dunoon and caused the vessel to heel right over and almost capsize.

Juno **(1937) off Craigmore 17th July 1937.** During the 1930s the LM&S/CSP combine went all out to become the dominant force on the Clyde and took advantage of falling construction prices caused by the Depression to virtually rebuild their Clyde fleet. The last large vessels to be introduced were two sisters, *Jupiter* and *Juno*, built in 1937. To the frustration of enthusiasts they continued with their owner's enthusiasm for hiding the paddles through the use of concealed boxes. They were also virtually identical. They were used on the basic services previously worked by *Duchess of Fife* and *Duchess of Rothesay* and were very effective replacements. To reflect the growth in car ownership and rising demand to transport such vehicles to the towns and resorts they were fitted with a space between the funnels to hold them. The transport of such vehicles in the 1930s was not for the faint hearted as vehicles had to be driven from shore to vessel over rather narrow planks when the tide allowed. A more efficient system had to wait until the 1950s.

Kenilworth (1898) passing Craigmore 17th July 1937. Under a great plume of smoke *Kenilworth* departs on another journey up the firth. By the number of fans displayed in her fan board she is obviously returning to her base at Craigendoran with calls at Innellan, Dunoon, Kirn and Kilcreggan. From the previous year, the North Bank vessels were repainted with the age old grained deckhouses, cream upperworks and black hulls being replaced by white upperworks and grey hulls. Clyde enthusiasts frequently tend to be rather conservative in attitudes and much disquiet was expressed at the idea of grey hulls. However, grey hulls had previously been worn by vessels of the G&SWR fleet prior to the grouping of 1923 and these were not the subject of controversy. Whether enthusiasts liked the changes or not was immaterial as the owners obviously did and the new colour scheme was maintained up until the War.

Glen Rosa (1893) arriving Rothesay 17th July 1937. This former G&SWR vessel was used on a variety of routes in her early days but, after the Great War, she settled down to providing the Fairlie-Millport-Kilchattan Bay-Rothesay service each summer. With the introduction of new vessels by the LM&SR in the 1930s she was promoted to the Wemyss Bay to Millport service in 1934. However, with the introduction of *Jupiter* and *Juno* in 1937 another vessel reshuffle saw *Duchess of Fife* take up this station while *Queen-Empress* attended to the Fairlie service. However, rather than be withdrawn the *Rosa* was held on to and became spare vessel. She provided extra sailings when required and luggage runs and also introduced a new afternoon cruise from Gourock and Dunoon to Rothesay and the Kyles. In this photograph she can be seen struggling in to Rothesay carrying what looks like a full load of passengers and is heeling over to port as a consequence.

***Jupiter* (1937) slows down on the approach to Rothesay 17th July 1937.** The former G&SWR vessel *Jupiter* was withdrawn after the 1935 season but the name was repeated on one of the new ferry class paddlers introduced to Clyde service in 1937. These vessels were designed to replace *Duchess of Fife* and *Queen-Empress* on the railway connectional work from Gourock and Wemyss Bay to Dunoon, Rothesay and the Kyles of Bute. They were good looking vessels with a well-balanced profile and two well designed funnels but continued the new fashion of having disguised paddle boxes. They were provided with room for the conveyance of cars and although two class vessels, they each had only one Dining Saloon which was divided between the two classes. This avoided duplication and allowed more covered saloon space to be available. As they were designed to sail all year round this was an important improvement in design.

***Caledonia* (1934) in Rothesay Bay 17th September 1937.** When *Caledonia* was introduced she was designed as a dual purpose vessel in that she provided the basic train connectional sailings to and from the coast while also being able to operate cruises as well. In her first season she was utilised on the Afternoon Cruise roster in succession to *Jupiter* but from 1936 this was widened to taking the Arran via the Kyles roster and the Forenoon Kyles service. However, in September her role became somewhat wider in that she took her turn on the basic "bread and butter" services. By September the main season was over and traffic had fallen well away, the only busy days being at weekends and on the various Holiday Mondays. As can be seen in this photograph she is sailing virtually empty on what was definitely not a profitable sailing. This concentration of the bulk of the annual traffic into three months provided a headache in that services had to be maintained when the traffic offering made most of the sailings uneconomical.

Mercury* (1892) and *Kenilworth* (1898) at Rothesay September 1927.** During the main season Rothesay and Dunoon were the busiest piers on the Clyde with an almost constant procession of steamers arriving and leaving. More than one vessel would be alongside at the same time which gave the enthusiast ample scope to take shots of various vessels together. In this shot we have, on the left the LM&SR's ***Mercury lying at Berth 2 while the L&NER's ***Kenilworth*** is pulling away from Berth 1. The former will have arrived from Wemyss Bay and will shortly be leaving to return there while the latter is on her way back to Craigendoran. Both look empty because traffic was to Rothesay in the morning with very little leaving for the mainland. Later in the day that position would be reversed as day trippers left to return home. Such unidirectional traffic flows allowed crews several relatively quiet runs each day where they could catch their breath.

Columba* (1878) at Rothesay.** After having made her outward call at Rothesay, ***Columba can be seen beginning to move away on her daily sailing to the Kyles of Bute, Tarbert and Ardrishaig. On this occasion she is very busy with her decks crowded and passengers leaning out of every conceivable vantage point. Just behind her bridge, between the funnels, mail bags and bicycles are piled up with more on the promenade deck below: this would suggest that this is a holiday Saturday in July when many passengers are heading out for their annual break and exiles are returning to their home islands. Interestingly, the clock on the pier tower intimated that it is after 1100 which means that the old vessel is running behind schedule. MacBraynes on this route were sticklers for prompt timekeeping and her captain would need a good explanation for her lateness to mollify head office. Her lateness would in turn mean that ***Pioneer*** would be late leaving from West Loch Tarbert for Islay and the Oban bus would be late leaving Ardrishaig.

Columba* (1878) and *Duchess of Fife* (1903) in Rothesay Bay August 1929.** Restored to her traditional colour scheme, the perfect example of Victorian elegance, ***Columba steams majestically into Rothesay Bay on a rather dank day. It was always the case that on the outward journey the Ardrishaig steamer berthed at Berth No. 3 at the east end of Rothesay pier while on the inward journey she came alongside Berth No. 1 at the other end of the pier. This made it easier for the long vessel to arrive and leave as quickly as possible due to the demands of her timetable. Thus, every morning on her way into Rothesay she sailed very close to the promenade which allowed for excellent views and photographs of the noble vessel. As July moved into August the peak of the season had passed and her passenger number began to decline. In the days before the Great War August was the "society month" when she conveyed the aristocracy and their servants north to their Highland hunting lodges but the 1920s were the beginning of a more democratic age which led to a fall in this traffic.

Mercury* (1892) leaving Rothesay July 1931.** An interesting shot of the elegant ***Mercury sailing away from Rothesay. When built she was a flyer in the G&SWR fleet and operated their important forenoon sailing from Princes Pier to the Kyles of Bute. After the Great War the LM&SR demoted her to the basic sailings from Gourock and Wemyss Bay to Dunoon and Rothesay, usually partnering ***Duchess of Fife***. In her case she was based at Auchenlochan and operated a morning commuter sailing from the Kyles pier and Rothesay to Wemyss Bay, returning in the evening. In between she mostly sailed from Rothesay to Wemyss Bay but once a day she ventured on a round trip from Rothesay to Dunoon and Gourock. She continued as such until the end of the 1933 season when she was withdrawn and scrapped. Unusually, she retained her navigating bridge behind the funnel throughout her career.

King Edward (1901) slowing to berth at Rothesay August 1931. Upon the delivery of *King George V* to the Williamson fleet in September 1926 *King Edward* was transferred to the sailings out of Glasgow and took up the important 1000 sailing. That sailings direct from Glasgow were still popular is demonstrated by the fact that there is no deck space left at all in this picture. Even with the Depression beginning to take its toll on employment there were still many passengers who were only too eager to escape from the city for a day. In the foreground can be seen one of the ubiquitous rowing boats that could be hired from the prom for a short period of time. Not all who did so knew what they were doing and such vessels could be a menace to steamers trying to berth in a restricted space. One master always carried potatoes on the bridge which he happily lobbed at any such rowing boat which came too close!

Arran (1926) in Rothesay Bay 17th September 1932. Clyde Cargo Steamers were formed by the Admiralty during the Great War to safeguard cargo services on the Clyde and brought together four different owners. Originally it was meant to last for the duration of the conflict only but it continued into the 1920s and 1930s. In the mid 20s it embarked on a process of fleet rebuilding and two vessels were ordered in 1926. One of them was named *Arran* and was principally intended to serve the East Arran ports of Brodick, Lamlash and Whiting Bay. She was also utilised elsewhere as appropriate and in December 1932 she was employed on the Loch Fyne cargo service which included calls at Tarbert, Ardrishaig, Otter Ferry, Inveraray and also Skipness in Kintyre. While so employed she ran aground on Barmore Island almost on the same spot that MacBrayne's *Chevalier* had done in 1927. Sadly she was wrecked after a short career and was immediately replaced by a new vessel of the same name.

***Columba* (1878) powers away from Rothesay 16th September 1932.** This wonderful view shows the old vessel in all her glory as she strides away from Rothesay on her way back to Glasgow, sailing under a prodigious cloud of smoke. While such a view stirs the heart of any steam enthusiast it had precisely the opposite effect on the population of the locality who complained vociferously about the smoke nuisance. The various local authorities passed byelaws outlawing such practices and many a captain and chief engineer found themselves being hauled into the Police Court to be prosecuted for producing too much smoke. In the background can be seen no fewer than five sea going vessels laid up in the bay, a sad reminder of the effects on trade of the Great Depression. Many more such vessels were laid up in Glasgow, Greenock and the many anchorages throughout the Clyde.

Duchess of Rothesay* (1895) pulls away from Rothesay on 2nd September 1933.** ***Duchess of Rothesay was regarded by many as one of the most beautiful and useful paddlers built for Clyde service. Initially used by the CSP Co. as a cruise vessel on the Arran via the Kyles service, she spent most of her life serving Dunoon, Rothesay and the Kyles piers from Princes Pier, Gourock and Wemyss Bay in an all the year round basis. Having just left Rothesay she is probably heading towards the Kyles of Bute on the Forenoon Kyles sailing. On this her passengers would have the choice of some time ashore at Colintraive, Tighnabruaich or Auchenlochan. She was well regarded by her owners and in her last season of 1939 she was judged to be still capable of sailing on the Arran via the Kyles sailing. In the background among the laid up vessels can be seen an L&NER vessel, either ***Talisman*** or ***Kenilworth***, lying at a buoy in the bay.

***Caledonia* (1934) coming alongside at Rothesay June 1934.** Under the command of Captain James Robertson *Caledonia* glides into Rothesay with the bow of *Jupiter* behind her. In 1934 she was employed on the Afternoon Cruise roster which, on Mondays, Wednesdays and Fridays had her arriving back at Rothesay at around 1620. There she met up with *Jupiter* which had arrived from Largs, Fairlie, the Millport piers and Kilchattan Bay on the afternoon cruise and Kilchattan Bay Circular trip. It was fitting that they met up as such because *Caledonia* had replaced *Jupiter* on the cruise roster. Although it is only June *Caledonia*'s waterline is already pretty dirty compared to *Jupiter*'s; however, while the latter had only entered service in May, *Caledonia* had been in constant use since March. Being the new vessel meant that her owners intended to utilise her as much as possible. In the background is *Duchess of Fife* arriving at Craigmore.

***Eagle III* (1910) leaving Rothesay 31st August 1934.** For many years *Eagle III* had been employed on the busy 1100 sailing from Bridge Wharf to the Kyles of Bute but was replaced on it by *King Edward* in 1933. This led to the *Eagle* being demoted on to the 0930 sailing to Rothesay which returned from the Bute resort at the relatively early time of 1430 This was very much a relief sailing and on the inward passage was rarely particularly heavily loaded. Her original owners, Buchanan Steamers, were renowned for not wasting money unnecessarily in the construction of vessels which meant that they had a relatively cheap appearance and this was true of the *Eagle*. Nevertheless she was a successful vessel and invariably had the longest season of the Upriver steamers, usually appearing in service in April and sailing continuously until the end of September. Thereafter, she took her turn on the winter tender duty.

Mercury* (1934) leaving Rothesay 31st August 1934.** Two new vessels were added to the LM&SR fleet in 1934, one of which was given the name ***Mercury. In that year she was employed on the Midday Kyles roster which made her one of the busiest vessels in the fleet. Starting from Rothesay at 0645 she made an express sailing to Wemyss Bay before crossing light to Innellan for another sailing to Greenock (Princes Pier). At the time honoured time of 1025 she left for Gourock and all piers to Rothesay and the Kyles, returning around 1620. This was followed by a direct sailing to Dunoon which returned to Gourock for another round trip at 1800 to Dunoon and back. Finally, at 1940, she left Gourock for all piers to Rothesay to berth overnight. This made her crew one of the hardest worked in the fleet. In the background can be seen ***Eagle III*** at a buoy.

Mercury* (1934) pulls away from Rothesay September 1934.** *Mercury* was the first of the 1934 sisters to enter service and her arrival caused something of a sensation as her design was so radically different from the Victorian and Edwardian paddlers most people were used to. She seemed bigger, bulkier and had her paddles seemingly concealed as much as possible. However, the two sisters were not identical which generated much discussion as to which was the better looking of the two, with most agreeing that it was ***Mercury. Her funnel was deemed to be of a better design and appearance and her saloon windows seemed of more traditional design. It was a matter of great interest that two yards, presumably handed the same plans and general design, had produced vessels that were not identical. Whatever the public thought of the twins one point that could not be disputed was that both vessels were worthwhile additions to the Clyde fleet.

King George V* slowing for Rothesay pier 1st June 1935.** When built ***King George V was equipped with high pressure turbines with steam being obtained from two Yarrow water tube boilers. This installation was not a success and the boilers were replaced in 1929. Still she gave problems with the result that in 1935 she was fitted with a conventional double ended Scotch boiler. At the same time she received new funnels of a greater diameter and it is in this condition that she is shown in the photograph. The new funnels fitted served to greatly improve her appearance. She spent most of her time on the Inveraray service although, from time to time, she did put in an appearance at Campbeltown. Before the main season started she invariably had a few days sailing out of Glasgow on Glasgow Corporation charters to Lochgoilhead for children. Although not generally known at the time, this proved to be her last season sailing for Williamson.

Atalanta* (1906) arriving at Rothesay 8th August 1936 in her final season as a Clyde steamer. *Atalanta was a "one off" among the early Clyde turbine vessels in that she wasn't particularly fast or large and only had one funnel. The G&SWR used her on a variety of routes but by the time of the LM&SR she was mainly used as the second Arran vessel during the summer, partnering originally the paddler ***Glen Sannox*** and then her turbine successor of the same name. She survived as such until 1936 when she was superseded by the new ***Marchioness of Graham***. For that season she was relegated to the Fairlie-Millport-Kilchattan Bay-Rothesay service but was sold off to Lancashire owners thereafter. By the mid 1930s the route had become a home for time expired G&SWR vessels, her predecessor having been the paddler ***Jupiter***. During pre-war days Millport was served by two vessels, the Fairlie vessel operating on the traditional G&SWR timetable while another vessel served Millport from Wemyss on the traditional Caley route. However the two services were eventually integrated with the Fairlie vessel also calling at Wemyss Bay.

Kenilworth (1898) coming alongside at Rothesay 15th August 1936. Hosting a goodly number of passengers *Kenilworth* is swinging round to starboard to call at Berth No 3 at the east end of Rothesay pier. She spent her entire career performing on the basic service from Craigendoran to Dunoon and Rothesay and also to the Holy Loch piers morning and evening. In 1936 the L&NER set out to try and boost the number of passengers carried each year by introducing calls at Largs, a pier completely outside their normal operating sphere. At the same time they decided to get their vessels noticed by introducing a new colour scheme which dispended with the browns and blacks and instead introduced grey for the hull and white for the upperworks. This move was decidedly unpopular with traditionalists while others thought the brighter colours showed off the red, white and black funnels. Unfortunately the grey hull quickly became covered in rust marks which marred the effect somewhat.

Kenilworth (1898) approaching Rothesay 17th July 1937. On a calm, benevolent day a well filled *Kenilworth* approaches Craigmore. Beside her mast a seaman is preparing the heaving line to be thrown on to the pier. Unlike on modern vessels the passengers are free to stand right up to the bow and at the stern which must have proved a nuisance when the crew were trying to work. By the date, it is obviously during the Glasgow Fair when the city decamped to the coast on summer holiday. Many of her passengers disembarking at Rothesay would travel on the trams to the delights of the beach and entertainment of Ettrick Bay on the west of the island. This was the peak period of the year and good weather always brought out crowds that thronged the vessels and resorts and greatly enhanced the annual financial results. Conversely, bad weather greatly depressed traffic to the horror of the owners. In an average year, the LM&SR worked out that more traffic was carried during the month of July than in the previous six months combined.

Jupiter* (1937) leaving Rothesay 17th July 1937.** Having discharged her passengers ***Jupiter is now leaving Rothesay on a sailing to Innellan, Dunoon, Kirn, Hunter's Quay and Gourock. Apart from time set aside each morning for them to take on coal and be washed down the railway connection vessels were never given time to have a rest at a pier. Instead it was a case of load up and set off, arrive at the intermediate piers and ultimately at the destination, unload then load and then off again on another sailing. Compared to the cruise vessels which frequently had long spaces between calling points the connectional vessels were always hurrying to and fro and their crews were kept hard at it throughout each working day. The only respite was on each alternate Sunday when they were allowed time off at Ormidale. Even then however the crew would have been kept busy on cleaning and maintenance work to maintain the high standards required of an LM&SR vessel.

Glen Sannox* approaching Rothesay 4th June 1932.** The fast turbine ***Glen Sannox was built in 1925 for the Arran service from Ardrossan. Compared to ***King George V*** which followed in 1926 she seems positively old fashioned but her design made her an excellent carrier of passengers, cargo, vehicles and livestock. Normally she would spend from June to the end of September as the principal vessel serving Arran but 1932 was a strange year for her in that she was only employed as such from mid June to the end of August when she was laid up. She spent the early part of June largely spare and on this day she was employed on the Upper Firth. As the regular vessels there all did as they were supposed to that day it suggests she was employed in the conveyance of large special parties to and from Dunoon and Rothesay. This photograph well illustrates her strength and power.

***Duchess of Montrose* (1930) in the Kyles of Bute 1st July 1935.** This shot, taken from *Jeanie Deans* off Kilmichael in the West Kyle, shows *Duchess of Montrose* at her best. The sleek turbine is moving quickly to pass her L&NER competitor with her passengers lining the rails and willing her on. She is slicing through the water with her bow wave almost reaching up to the anchor. The *Montrose* introduced a whole new standard on the firth with being a one class ship only. This avoided the duplication of facilities and allowed her designers to produce a vessel with excellent accommodation to suit all weathers. In 1934 her outward appearance was greatly enhanced with the provision of a full length mainmast to replace the stump she carried in her original condition. Now people had to look carefully to distinguish her from *Duchess of Hamilton*. Her success greatly exceeded anything her owners expected and she had virtually paid for herself by this time.

***Marmion* (1906) steaming through the Kyles 16th September 1932.** *Marmion* was built, as was common for the NBR, at the Inglis yard at Pointhouse and was designed as an all year round workhorse, being utilised mostly on routes to Rothesay and the Kyles. Like the LM&SR *Duchess of Fife* she was in commission for most of the year and proved to be a robust vessel. During the winter the L&NER employed two vessels at a time in service. The first was based at Garelochhead and spent the day serving the piers on the Gareloch and crossing to Princes Pier. The other vessel was Ardnadam based and maintained the morning and evening service from the Holy Loch to Craigendoran as well as serving the Cowal piers and Rothesay. Unlike their South Bank competitors the L&NER made no attempt to provide Sunday sailings in winter. With the appearance of the new *Talisman* in 1935 *Marmion* found herself being relegated to Bowling Harbour during subsequent winters.

Eagle III (1910) in the Kyles of Bute 4tn April 1931. This photograph was taken from *King Edward* and shows *Eagle III* following her down the East Kyles of Bute. In the background to the left can be seen the towers that marked the Narrows while on the right is Colintraive pier. Given the month it is obviously Easter when almost a full Summer set of sailings was provided to cater for Glasgow holidaymakers. By the looks of it the turbine has creamed off the bulk of the traffic leaving the paddler to deal with what remained. As both vessels headed down towards Rothesay we can be sure that *Eagle* will fall further and further behind the turbine leaving her passengers to contemplate the wisdom of their choice of vessel. On many occasions passengers on *Eagle* had the pleasure of being overhauled by other Williamson vessels on the way home that had left Rothesay much later than they had!

Waverley **(1899) in the Kyles 1931.** Having provided the daily sailing from Craigendoran to Tighnabruaich and Auchenlochan *Waverley* is on the homeward journey in the East Kyle and is making for Port Bannatyne and then Rothesay where more passengers will join her. As is obvious her Kyles cruise has been very lightly patronised. During service in the Great War her bow was raised up to the promenade deck and this alteration was maintained when she returned to the Clyde. In 1933 deck saloons were fitted fore and aft on the promenade deck. She did not sail in 1939 but was called up for war duty in that year and found herself at Dunkirk in 1940. Having made several crossings her luck ran out and she was sunk on the way home. In a bitter irony many of the troops she had on board were from Glasgow and had recognised her when boarding. Sadly, the loss of life at Dunkirk was heavy.

Marchioness of Graham **(1936) steaming through the Kyles of Bute June 1936.** The "new girl" of 1936 was designed primarily to maintain the winter service to Arran and be the secondary vessel to the island during the summer timetable. Although bigger and heavier she had a passing resemblance to *Marchioness of Lorne* of the previous year and was quite pleasing to the eye. Given what her intended route was, she was provided with plenty of deck space to store cargo, motor cars and livestock which meant she had only one saloon on the promenade deck. However, plenty of covered seating was provided on the main and lower decks. She is heeling over in the photograph although not carrying a heavy load of passengers which suggests she has been on the Midday Kyles roster and is turning quickly round after leaving Auchenlochan. In the early season she was regularly used to fill gaps on other services while charter and special party sailings were being undertaken.

***Glen Rosa* (1893) approaching Keppel 9th August 1934.** This photograph shows the everyday scene of *Glen Rosa* coming out of the Millport piers heading for Largs. It was actually taken from *Duchess of Montrose* which that day was heading for Stranraer and called at Keppel at 1035. *Glen Rosa* is on the 1020 sailing from Millport Old which called at Keppel just ahead of the *Montrose*, at 1027. After making a call at Largs she would then have carried on to Wemyss Bay for the main train connection to Glasgow. In 1934 the *Rosa* had been "promoted" to being the main Millport steamer while *Jupiter* (1896) replaced her on the Fairlie-Millport service. Keppel Pier is well known as being the Cumbrae calling point of the larger excursion vessels but, before the war, virtually every vessel sailing to and from Millport and Kilchattan Bay also called in as traffic for the east end of the town found it easier to use than having to traipse round the bay to the Old Pier.

***Glen Sannox* (1925) leaving Largs 31st July 1932.** Although designated as the main Arran steamer each summer *Glen Sannox* was allowed to wander and provided evening cruises from the Arran ports and afternoon cruises between Arran sailings. Another favourite duty was carrying charter parties on Sundays from Ardrossan and Millport. Among such sailings were Health and Wellbeing sailings from these ports up the firth. In this photograph she is thus engaged as it is a Sunday and she has a huge crowd on board. *Glen Sannox* was always regarded as distinctly old fashioned looking as she had so obviously been designed as another *Duchess of Argyll* but the truth of the matter was that she was well suited for her role and had plenty of space for cargo, livestock and motor vehicles as well as a large number of passengers. The most obvious difference between the vessels was that the *Sannox* had a wooden bridge while that of the *Argyll* was canvas.

Duchess of Hamilton (1932) in the Largs Channel. When **Duchess of Hamilton** was delivered in 1932 and put on the cruises out of Ayr, Troon and Ardrossan she was regarded with great suspicion by regular travellers from the Ayrshire Coast who were unhappy at the withdrawal of the popular **Juno** from the station. However, the clever idea of transferring **Juno**'s crew to the newcomer, the attractions of the vessel herself and the greater variety of cruises offered soon won them over. As well as providing a bewildering range of cruising possibilities from Ayr most of her cruises arrived at resorts like Largs, Dunoon and Rothesay in the early afternoon and this allowed a variety of afternoon cruises to be advertised. Coupled with other sailings in the intensive LM&SR network the passenger of the day was presented with an amazing number of cruising possibilities in any one day. She proved to be a very successful vessel in the 1930s but some enthusiasts always regarded her as the poor relation of **Duchess of Montrose**.

Talisman (1935) off Cumbrae on an Evening Cruise 18th August 1935. If the L&NER could be accused of being old fashioned in the design of **Jeanie Deans** in 1931 they certainly more than made up for it with their next new vessel, **Talisman**, built in 1935. She was the first direct-acting diesel electric paddle vessel in the world and the largest diesel electric paddle vessel. Her arrival on the Clyde generated copious interest from both the general public and the professional world and gained such publicity that must have made the management thrilled. In appearance however, she looked relatively normal although the solid bulwarks at the bow were certainly not an asset. She was designed to maintain the Kyles of Bute sailing in the summer and the Ardnadam/Dunoon/Rothesay service in winter and was very successful on the latter because of how she greatly reduced the running costs of a lightly used roster.

Wee Cumbrae* (1935) off Keppel 18th August 1935.** Having got wind of a plan by a private company to initiate a ferry service on a small vessel from Largs to Millport, the LM&SR moved quickly to get in first by building their own vessel. Thus the 60 passenger ***Wee Cumbrae entered service in 1935. When originally introduced she had two small saloons and a very restricted space on deck amidships for passengers which made her somewhat uncomfortable when busy. However, in 1936, deck railings were fitted and passengers were given more space on her promenade deck. Her service was a supplement to the existing steamer services to Millport and also operated late into the evening. In 1935 her sailings were not listed in the main LM&SR steamer timetable and were only advertised locally. However, from 1936, they were included in the summer timetable. At busy times her sailings siphoned off traffic from the larger vessels and provided more flexibility to the travelling public.

***Glen Rosa* (1893) leaving Millport 18th July 1931.** *Glen Rosa* is seen here setting out from Millport bound for the mainland with Little Cumbrae dead ahead. Millport Old Pier was not the easiest of piers to use as it required the vessel having to warp round the pier in some way. A steamer coming in from the south would approach the pier then turn sharply to port to berth at the side of the pier, keeping a wary eye on the shore straight ahead. On departure she would have to warp round the front of the pier to then leave on a straight course south. If the tide was right a vessel could sail between the islands in the bay and then turn to port to berth at the front of the pier, thus giving her a straight course out when she left. For these reasons the larger turbines usually used Keppel to save time, the fact that passengers had to walk some distance from the town to get to Keppel obviously being considered as of no importance!

Glen Rosa (1893) approaching Brodick 11th August 1931. *Glen Rosa* was a handsome vessel but with an unusual design in that she had a short, raised foredeck, a design she shared with her sister *Minerva*. This was to facilitate her use on the winter service to Arran on which her passengers were invariably treated to a lively and memorable journey! In the summer months she served on the Fairlie to Millport, Kilchattan Bay and Rothesay service on which she became known as the "Bob Yacht" because of the cheap afternoon cruise she operated to the Bute capital with time ashore. Seeing her at Brodick in the summer was therefore unusual but, for periods in 1930 and 1931, she swapped places with *Atalanta* and became the secondary Arran vessel. She was replaced at Millport in 1937 and for two seasons became the "odds and sods" vessel operating relief and luggage sailings. In 1938, in conjunction with the Empire Exhibition at Bellahouston, she operated special late sailings to Dunoon and Rothesay.

Davaar (1885) steams away from Lochranza 14th August 1931. Heeling over to port because of a gale *Davaar* has left Lochranza bound for Gourock and Glasgow. Once clear of the loch she would turn to starboard and head for Garroch Head on Bute after which her course would be altered to take her north up the Sound of Bute and on to Cloch Point. At the stern several passengers can be seen waving handkerchiefs at relatives or friends on the pier. The vessel is carrying a good number of passengers who no doubt are at the end of their summer holiday and would leave the vessel at Gourock to catch the train to Glasgow where they would arrive home in the early afternoon. What a glorious way to end a holiday!

***Davaar* (1885) leaving Lochranza 7th September 1932.** The graceful and elegant *Davaar* has been captured in the process of reversing out of Lochranza on her up run from Campbeltown to Glasgow. In the normal course of events she would head direct to Gourock where she would be expected at 1200. After this she would head for Princes Pier for another train connection, this time to Glasgow St. Enoch station, and then up the river to the Broomielaw at Clyde Street. The afternoon would then be spent unloading whatever cargo had come from Arran and Kintyre and then starting to load the assorted boxes, crates, packages and the like for the coast. The following morning her crew would be roused very early and she would sail at 0600 to return to Campbeltown. Over the course of a year the Campbeltown steamers would cover a very large mileage in service and each would do it for eleven months with the remaining time off for overhaul and survey.

***Queen Alexandra* (1912) at Lochranza 23rd June 1930.** The first route operated by turbine steamers on the Clyde was to Campbeltown in Kintyre. For many years townsfolk wanted the service improved and welcomed the new type of vessel with open arms. The regular steamer on the route in the late 1920s and early 1930s was *Queen Alexandra* and she left Princes Pier at 0845 and Gourock at 0905 and called at Dunoon, Wemyss Bay, Fairlie, Lochranza and Campbeltown to arrive at 1300. Nearly two hours were given ashore before she returned by the same piers to arrive back at Princes Pier at 1850. At her stern can be seen *Dalriada* on the daily passenger and cargo service to Kintyre. Williamson and the Campbeltown Co. competed fiercely on the route but many preferred travelling at the more leisurely pace of the latter.

Queen-Empress* (1912) approaching Lochranza 7th September 1932.** We can see ***Queen-Empress arriving at Lochranza on her way to Campbeltown in the gloom of an autumn day. Each September she was employed on the route in the place of ***Queen Alexandra*** as the traffic did not merit the use of the larger vessel. She operated a slowed down service to match her more leisurely speed so this might not have allowed passengers to sample the delights of a trip to Machrihanish in a train of the Campbeltown & Machrihanish Light Railway. This practice of substituting a paddler for the turbine in September continued on the Campbeltown route right up to the late 1960s. ***Queen-Empress*** also made an appearance at Campbeltown on the evening of Glasgow Fair Friday in mid July when a relief sailing was provided from Fairlie to cope with the holiday crowds.

Dalriada* (1926) canting at Campbeltown June 1930.** From the 1820s on, the ports of the Kintyre peninsula received a daily service, with the exception of Sundays, to and from Glasgow operated by vessels of the impressively named Campbeltown & Glasgow Steam Packet Joint Stock Co. Ltd. Apart from the overhaul period during the winter one vessel would leave Glasgow while another duly set off from Campbeltown. Additional sailings were provided at peak times while some cruising was also fitted in. The last vessel built for the Company was ***Dalriada which distinguished herself by being the fastest single screw vessel of the period in the world. She further distinguished herself by having an exceedingly tall funnel. In this shot she has discharged at Campbeltown and is being warped round to face the sea ready for a quick start the following day. Note the long warping line stretching from the bow to the pier. With simultaneous orders to the engine room to go astern and then ahead and to the seamen on the winches the long vessel would slowly come round and reberth at the pier.

***Davaar* (1885) looking aft June 1929.** An interesting shot taken onboard a Campbeltown steamer in which we can see the seaman on the wheel peering forward while the officer of the watch appears fascinated by something behind the vessel. We can see the cargo cradle sitting on top of the forward hold and directly below the bridge is the cargo hold hoist, an innovative feature in its time. A passenger leans on the hold rail watching what is ahead. The number of passengers carried varied between the seasons with some summer sailings being very busy. They were afforded full facilities with saloons and a dining saloon serving what were apparently excellent meals. While this shot appears to have been taken on a relatively idyllic day in the summer the weather was frequently very different in the winter and what few passengers that were aboard could look forward to days of exceedingly rough seas rounding Garroch Head and on coming down the Kilbrannan Sound.

Aboard *Dalriada* (1926) looking aft from the foredeck June 1929. This wonderful and rare shot provides an indication of what it would have been like to travel on *Dalriada* in the early days of her life. Taken from towards the bow it shows the forward hold with cargo handling facilities, the bridge with the master supervising events from the wing, her builder's plaque, the base of her enormous funnel and scattered in the midst of it some seating for passengers. Anyone attempting to sit there when the cargo handling equipment was being used would have had a noisy time of it! She is alongside at Carradale in Kintyre and cargo is being manhandled amidships; note the trolley with fish boxes ready for loading. On her daily sailing goods of all shapes and sizes would have been handled alongside various forms of livestock and some passengers. Intermediate calls were carried out as quickly as possible and would have provided endless fascination for her passengers.

***Davaar* (1885) canting at Campbeltown June 1929.** It's an unusual point to claim that a rebuilding greatly enhanced a vessel's appearance but this was particularly true of *Davaar*. When built she had two funnels and alleyways round her aft saloon but in 1903 she was reboilered and was fitted with only one funnel of a larger size than each of the originals while her saloon was widened to full width. After a career of being the extra and cruise vessel she settled down to the bread and butter work of carrying passengers, livestock and cargo to and from the Kintyre peninsula. Such were her graceful lines that at times it was difficult to remember that she was a working ship rather than a rich man's yacht. Sadly, the graceful vessel had an ignominious end. After being withdrawn from service in October 1939 she was briefly returned in January 1940 to replace the requisitioned *Dalriada* but was withdrawn again in March and later taken over to be a block ship at Newhaven. While avoiding that fate she was eventually beached and broken up in 1943.

Campbeltown Quay on 4th September 1932 with *Davaar* (1885) and *Killarney* (1893). This photograph, taken from the Royal Hotel, provides a fascinating insight into the workings of the Kintyre port. On the left lies *Davaar* which by the lack of obvious activity has finished working cargo and passengers. At the face of the pier is *Killarney* calling on one of her periodic Scottish cruises. Her passengers are obviously ashore and some of her crew are taking their ease leaning over her rail. At the back of the quay numerous fishing boats are lying, resting after a night's work on the firth while a small cargo vessel is along the side of the pier. At the head of the East Quay lie more non-local vessels while the lifeboat is tucked up inside the harbour. On the quay itself are stacked an enormous number of barrels, some of which will be for fish while others will contain the "Water of Life" from the local distillery. Add on onlookers taking it all in and you have an evocative scene of everyday life in the 1930s.

King George V* (1926) at Campbeltown 12th August 1934.** Rather unusually, the ship is berthed bow to shore across the pier end. While the Campbeltown Co. vessels were the mainstay of services to the Kintyre port from 1901 they had competition from the fleet of Turbine Steamers who provided a daily service to Lochranza and Campbeltown from the railheads of Princes Pier, Gourock, Wemyss Bay and Fairlie, creaming off a large part of the traffic in the process. Originally operated by ***King Edward the service was normally provided by the first and second ***Queen Alexandras*** so the sight of ***King George*** is somewhat unusual. Normally the 1926 built vessel operated on their other service to Inveraray but on occasion, the vessels did change round. Behind her can be seen the masts of ***Davaar*** which has arrived from Glasgow. In a race the turbine would have left her far behind but many passengers did continue to use ***Dalriada*** and ***Davaar***, partly out of local loyalty but the fact their fares were cheaper could have been an influencing factor!

Queen-Empress* (1912) leaving Campbeltown 7th June 1930.** One of the most useful "Maids of all Work" built for the Upriver services was ***Queen-Empress, delivered to John Williamson in 1912. Originally used on the Glasgow to Rothesay and Kyles route she was frequently utilised on other routes and on special cruises originating from such piers as Princes Pier and Helensburgh. Normally she took over the Campbeltown route of ***Queen Alexandra*** during the quieter month of September but did visit the Kintyre port at other times either because she was standing in for the larger vessel because of charter commitments or on one of her special Coast cruises. Such a cruise would take her to Campbeltown from such piers as Hunters Quay, Kirn, Innellan, Kilchattan Bay or Tighnabruaich, piers not served by the turbine steamer. When the company was taken over by the LM&SR in 1937 she was transferred to railway connectional sailings and finished up on the Fairlie to Millport, Kilchattan Bay and Rothesay service

Queen Alexandra **(1912) departing from Campbeltown 27th June 1930.** *Queen Alexandra* was the third turbine steamer to be built for Williamson and the second to be named *Queen Alexandra*. Launched in 1912 she spent virtually all of her Williamson peacetime life maintaining the Campbeltown service. After overnighting in the Albert Harbour, Greenock she started her day at Princes Pier at 0845 and called at Gourock, Dunoon, Wemyss Bay and Fairlie before heading for the north of Arran to make a stop at Lochranza. She continued down the Kilbrannan Sound to Pirnmill and then Campbeltown where her travellers were given nearly two hours ashore. They could also travel across to the west of Kintyre to Machrihanish on the light railway. To the right of the ship's bow can be seen the Campbeltown Shipyard. Sadly, all that can now be discerned of this enterprise is the remains of a slipway. While at Campbeltown she would normally have been joined by either *Davaar* or *Dalriada*.

Columba **(1878) alongside at Tarbert September 1934.** The mighty *Columba* calls at Tarbert on her way to Ardrishaig and unloads what looks like a small number of passengers. Some others are remaining on board for the sail up Loch Fyne to Ardrishaig where a bus will be waiting to convey passengers on to Oban. The photograph gives an impression of just how long the vessel was; for many years she was the longest Clyde steamer and was also the first to be built of steel. Such was her length that the pier at Tarbert had to be extended to cope with her and for generations it was known as the "*Columba Pier*". The promenade deck was immense and, when built, was mostly unencumbered with any restrictions but as the years passed various alterations were made including extending the bridge and building housings for lifejackets. The photo clearly shows the rings upon her funnel because, in her early days, the fleet sported a black ring upon the red. There is a decided "end of season" feeling to the scene with the paint of her funnels having lost their sheen and the paucity of passengers.

A deck view onboard *King George V* (1926) looking forward from the after deck. This excellent shot conveys what it must have been like to be on a busy Clyde steamer sailing down the firth on a cruise. In it we can clearly see one of the many innovations introduced by this vessel such as the enclosing of the sides of the promenade deck to form a sheltered seating area. Thus more sheltered seating with a view was made available to passengers. On this day the weather is such that many of her passengers prefer to sit outside in the sun. The fact that she is dressed overall gives a clue to what was important about the day. It was 6th May 1935, the 25th anniversary of the accession of King George V and special cruises were organised to cater for it was a national holiday. The ***George*** was bound for Inveraray and has just rounded Toward Point on her way into Rothesay. Such holidays were a bonus to the steamer companies as they produced much heavier traffic than would have been expected at that time of year.

King George V* (1926) at Inveraray 8th September 1930.** Here we see an empty looking ***King George V lying quietly alongside the pier at Inveraray while her passengers enjoy time ashore. By that time the peak season had passed so we can assume that she will not have carried a large number of passengers. An interesting feature of Turbine Steamers was that in September the Campbeltown turbine was replaced by a paddler, no doubt to reflect the relative lack of traffic whereas Inveraray held on to its turbine right to the end of the season. Whether this signified the traffic held up more or whether no other vessel was available is unknown but it remained a feature until 1935. Thus the ***George*** would not join ***Queen Alexandra*** in winter lay-up until after the Glasgow Autumn Holiday. For her crew this would have been welcomed as it provided several more weeks of paid employment for most of them.

***Minard* (1926) and *King George V* (1926) lying at Inveraray 1935.** This evocative photograph illustrates the cargo vessel *Minard* and the revolutionary turbine *King George V* lying together at Inveraray on the 25th anniversary of King George V's accession on 6th May 1935. Both vessels are dressed overall for the occasion while bunting is also strung up on the pier. The turbine has arrived on a special holiday excursion from the upper firth ports while the cargo vessel appears to be slumbering in the sunshine. As it was a national holiday it is quite possible that *Minard* has had her single trip to Glasgow cancelled for the day. Although both vessels were built in the same year it would be difficult to think of two vessels more unalike. Berthed at the back of the pier we can see the vessel used on the ferry service to St. Catherine's across the loch. Taken together, the view epitomises a sunny Clydeside day in the 1930s.

Lochfyne (1931) and *Glencoe* (1846) berthed at the Broomielaw 4th June 1931. It would be extremely difficult to imagine a combination of vessels so completely different than what we have here. Nearest the quay is the newest ship in the MacBrayne fleet, newly out of the builder's yard. The diesel electric **Lochfyne** encapsulates the new world of the 1930s with her innovative motive power, her strictly utilitarian appearance and her onboard comforts. On the outside lies **Glencoe**, the oldest vessel in the fleet. Built in 1846 and with her original steeple engine still in place, she represented the world of the early Victorian era and the early days of steam navigation. Compared to the spaciousness and airiness of the new vessel, she was dark, cramped and Dickensian. Visitors moving from one ship to the other were very much moving between two different worlds.

Lochness (1929) on the river July 1929. The new vessel is seen leaving Harland & Wolff's yard to undergo trials on the firth. Her entry in full service was not as straightforward as one would have wished and after sailing from Glasgow to Tarbert as relief to **Columba** at Glasgow Fair she returned to her builders to allow several important issues to be dealt with. Because of this her actual entry into full service at Stornoway was delayed until August. Within a year or two of entering service a major cosmetic change was made to her with the lengthening of her funnel. In this photograph the funnel appears rather squat and resembled the sort of funnel fitted to **Lochearn** and **Lochmor** the following year. One assumes this meant it had the delightful habit of covering the top deck and its passengers with soot and smuts! Whatever the reason, the alteration improved her looks. Behind are the Govan Graving Docks and Princes Dock.

Lochness **(1929) in the upper river July 1929.** This historic shot shows *Lochness* passing her builders on the day of her trials in July 1929. Having been completed to the builder's satisfaction, the new ship then had to run trials to make sure everything worked as it was designed to and that she was capable of being given a certificate to enter service. Trials of a new ship were a trying time for all, with the shipyard hoping that she could fulfil what was expected of her by the owners while the latter decided whether to accept her or not. Designed to serve Stornoway, her first actual sailing was on Glasgow Fair Saturday in mid July when she duplicated *Columba* from Glasgow to Tarbert. She must have been some sight alongside the Loch Fyne pier. Thereafter, it was August before she began on her intended service where she was given a rapturous welcome.

Columba **(1878) and** *Iona* **(1864) being broken up at Dalmuir 21 March 1936.** After careers of 58 and 72 years respectively the two famous old ships were withdrawn from service after the 1935 summer season. After spending the winter laid up in the East India Harbour in Greenock both vessels were sold in March 1936 to Arnott, Young and Co. of Dalmuir to be broken up and were towed to the yard for demolition to take place. The work was carried out quickly and as can be seen after a matter of weeks *Iona* has virtually disappeared with only the hull left while *Columba* has been internally stripped with the funnels, mast and promenade deck disappearing. Many people requested part of the vessels which the company was happy to supply and these found their way to many points across the globe. It can safely be said that their passing was truly the end of an era.

Mountaineer (1910) and Lucy Ashton (1888) laid up in Bowling Harbour 1928. For many years unneeded vessels in the winter were laid up in Bowling Harbour when not required. Thus, one would have found vessels from MacBrayne, the L&NER and Williamson-Buchanan lying sedately awaiting the return of summer. However, vessels of the LM&SR were always laid up in Greenock, usually the Albert Harbour. The vessel in the foreground in this photograph is MacBrayne's **Mountaineer** with **Lucy Ashton** inside her. **Mountaineer** was used during the winter to relieve **Comet** on the Lochgoilhead route, **Lochinvar** on the Sound of Mull, **Pioneer** on the Islay service and on the Portree service but had several months of inactivity to look forward to. Vessels laid up usually had their deckseats removed for maintenance but on **Mountaineer** they are still in position but covered by tarpaulins. When she was required steam would need to be raised and the vessel hosed down but her seats were already in position, not that they would have been heavily used by passengers in the dead of winter!

Lochiel (1906) in Bowling Harbour 20th May 1930. MacBrayne have always been great believers in recycling ship's names and in the case of **Lochiel** there have been no fewer than four of them serving in West Highland waters. The vessel illustrated here was the third of the name and was awarded to the Company in 1919 by the Shipping Controller. Although she carried a small amount of passenger accommodation she was essentially a cargo vessel and was principally used on the Stornoway cargo service from Glasgow although she did have spells on the Islay cargo service. Later in her career she became a relief cargo vessel used to relieve others for overhaul or to undertake special cargo and livestock sailings. The fact that she is laid up at Bowling suggests she was resting between spells of service relieving. Behind her can be seen the funnel of an L&NER vessel, possibly **Waverley**.

Pioneer (1905) arriving in the West Loch 15th August 1931. *Pioneer* was a neat little vessel which spent the bulk of her life serving Islay. She was specially designed for the service which required a vessel of shallow draught to be able to berth at West Loch Tarbert Pier at all states of the tide. An unusual feature of her design was the very small paddles, a feature she shared with *Mountaineer*. She was rostered to sail from Port Ellen on Mondays, Wednesday and Fridays via Gigha to West Loch Tarbert and then from there to Craighouse on Jura and Port Askaig. En route she also called at the ferry on the north of Gigha. On the other weekdays she reversed this routing and spent the weekends at Port Ellen. The Islay service was a traditional mail boat service with the vessel expected to carry cargo and livestock as well as passengers so it seems strange that she was not fitted with cargo handling gear.

Pioneer (1905) paddles up the West Loch 8th September 1932. As part of the fleet replacement programme MacBrayne ordered a new vessel in 1938 to replace *Pioneer*. This vessel, given the name *Lochiel*, materialised in 1939 and took the service over while *Pioneer* was transferred to Oban to carry out a programme of short cruises. Unfortunately, nobody in management seemed to have considered whether the new, larger, vessel could cope with the West Loch Pier and she soon came to grief with a damaged propeller and sundry other bashes and dents. The result was that *Pioneer* was hastily brought back while the newer vessel retreated to Oban and it was 1940 before the rebuilding of the pier enabled her to take over the service. Thereafter *Pioneer* was used in a variety of roles before being taken over by the Admiralty who, at the end of the war, bought her outright. Thus, *Pioneer* disappeared from her native waters and was the last paddle steamer used on regular MacBrayne Hebridean services. Obvious in this photograph is the wash. *Pioneer* is not running fast, but her drag in the shallow West Loch has created a lovely wave pattern.

Pioneer* (1905) alongside at West Loch Tarbert in the early 1930s.** Having arrived from Islay ***Pioneer can be seen berthed at her mainland terminal. She has discharged a large number of mail bags which are being loaded into a lorry for transport to East Loch Tarbert pier to be loaded on to ***Columba*** for the journey to Gourock and Glasgow. Also on the pier can be seen a wonderful collection of old coaches which would carry any passengers desirous of catching ***Columba***. The timetable intimated that passengers could walk between the piers but this would have required a certain nimbleness to achieve in the time allowed! This time honoured system of connections from the Central Belt to Islay and associated islands survived until the 1970s when the less romantic system of a connection by coach from Glasgow took over the job. On busy days the coaches had to make several journeys between the piers to make sure that everybody got to where they should have been.

Pioneer* (1905) berthed at West Loch Tarbert.** If one wanted to build a pier in an inaccessible place difficult to berth at it would have been difficult to produce anything that would have beaten West Loch Tarbert. Situated right at the top of the loch in shallow water the pier head was extremely small. To berth, the vessel had to steam up until off the pier when ropes were passed ashore. The vessel then had to be turned around using a combination of the ropes and the engines so that she passed through 180 degrees before slowly coming alongside to begin discharging. At low spring tides the vessel was barely afloat while this positioning was carried out. All being well she was allowed around 90 minutes to do this, discharge and then load up again. On Glasgow Fair Saturday she required the help of ***Mountaineer to cope with the traffic and it must have been some sight to see both vessels in such a restricted space at the same time. While passengers found the berthing fascinating the romance was probably lost on ***Pioneer***'s master!

Lochiel (1906) approaching Bruichladdich. Although built in 1906 *Lochiel* only joined the MacBrayne fleet in 1919, having previously being named *Devonia* and employed from Plymouth to Guernsey and St Brieux. For MacBrayne she sailed principally on the cargo services and was a well kent sight on the Stornoway run although she did make appearances on the Glasgow to Islay route. While the mail service from West Loch Tarbert concentrated on Port Ellen and Port Askaig, the cargo vessels called at a variety of points, one of which was Bruichladdich, a port famed for its distillery and its product. The round trip from Glasgow usually took a week to accomplish. In this exceptionally rare image we can see that her masts bear extensions; these were to facilitate the fitting of a wireless aerial. Latterly the vessel was spare and was sold out of the fleet in 1938 and, after the Second World War, eventually ended up in Greece.

Plover (1904) leaving Oban 25th March 1932. Having reversed out of the pier, *Plover* is going ahead while turning to starboard to cross Oban Bay on the way out. Although a small vessel in size, *Plover* had full passenger facilities including sleeping accommodation. From 1931 on, *Plover* normally replaced *Fusilier* on the Mallaig to Portree service during the winter. With the delivery of *Lochnevis* in 1934 she was rendered surplus and withdrawn from service. However, she was far from finished and was refitted at Ardrossan into something altogether more luxurious. She was renamed *Loch Aline* and became the Directors' yacht, carrying them on annual summer cruises in the islands. For that she had a yellow funnel. However, she still carried out relieving duties during which her funnel was repainted red and black. In 1918 she made a name for herself by engaging with a German submarine, firing her gun at it and causing it to submerge. Mercifully, passages to Barra thereafter tended to be quieter affairs!

Plover **(1904) reversing out of Oban 25th March 1932.** This vessel was of great fascination in that the ship herself and her engines were of different ages. MacBrayne was not a company that believed in wasting anything and when ***Flowerdale*** was wrecked off Lismore in 1904 her engines and boilers were salvaged and, considered to be eminently useful, one engine and one boiler were fitted to ***Plover*** thus saving the Company some money in building costs. She was designed for service from Oban, Mallaig and Kyle of Lochalsh to the Inner and Outer Isles and remained as such until replaced by the new sisters of 1930, ***Lochmor*** and ***Lochearn***. Many are the tales told of horrendous passages on the old vessel in bad weather but she was considered to be an excellent sea boat. After 1930 she was still used to relieve the new vessels for annual overhaul. With her cramped accommodation she appeared to be from another planet compared to the 1930 twins!

120

Lochfyne* (1931) alongside the North Pier, Oban 1st August 1931.** The new feature of Oban in 1931 was the arrival of a new vessel for the Staffa and Iona excursion. Painted in the new colours of grey hull ***Lochfyne sailed on a daily basis from Oban to Staffa and Iona. Three days a week she set out via the Sound of Mull while on the other three she went via the Ross of Mull. In each case passengers had around an hour ashore on both Staffa and Iona and got a cruise Round Mull into the bargain. In the 1930s MacBrayne became experts at advertising the attractions of their services and waxed lyrical in their timetable/guidebook about the various attractions that visitors would experience on their vessels. Under the Sacred Isle tour it was said that, when the ship got underway, nothing could be heard bar "the lapping of the water against the hull". The author was obviously hard of hearing for, on ***Lochfyne***, quite a lot could be heard such as the whines coming from her engines and the sounds of vibration throughout the ship! That being said, she did prove popular with the travelling public. The vacant land behind ***Lochfyne***'s stern is now occupied by the cathedral which was built in 1938.

Iona* (1864) arriving at Oban 1st August 1931.** After the loss of the ***Grenadier in 1926 and the ***Chevalier*** in 1927, ***Iona*** was transferred from the Clyde to Oban to maintain the Fort William service. In pre-war days this was not so much a cruise as it was after 1945 but rather was a service which served as an important link in the Royal Route from Glasgow to Inverness and connected into the ***Gondolier*** on the Caledonian Canal. Several sailings were made a day with several nights being spent at Fort William. Calls were also made at Lismore, Appin, Kentallen and Ardgour. Inverness passengers used the train from Fort William to Banavie to connect with ***Gondolier***. In all, the full journey took two days. In the background we can see ***Mountaineer*** lying off waiting for space at the North Pier and a large luxury yacht anchored off Kerrera.

***Lochmor* (1930) alongside at the North Pier, Oban 2nd August 1931.** Although intended for the Outer Isles service from Kyle of Lochalsh and Mallaig *Lochmor* did, at times, replace her sister *Lochearn* on the Inner Isles service. On this she gave three sailings a week from Oban to Tobermory, Kilchoan, Coll, Tiree, Castlebay on Barra and Lochboisdale on South Uist. At the latter she connected with her sister thus giving her passengers the chance of sailing on to Lochmaddy, Tarbert and, once a week in summer, Dunvegan on Skye. In the 1930s the Inner Isles vessel was based at the North Pier and in the photograph shore staff are working her cargo handling equipment while her crew take a well-earned rest. Astern of her can be seen a number of steam drifters which were probably engaged on the herring fishing for which they moved round the coast as the shoals of fish moved.

***Mountaineer* (1910) and *Lochearn* (1930) at Oban North Pier 3rd August 1931.** In this atmospheric photograph we see *Mountaineer* returning to Oban from one of her frequent cruises. By the 1930s her role was to provide short morning and afternoon cruises from Oban for the benefit of holidaymakers. In the mornings her destinations included Tobermory, Loch Sunart, Crinan and Fort William and usually arrived back around 1445. These were then followed by shorter afternoon cruises which could take her to Loch Spelve, Loch Creran and Loch Corry. She also fitted in several sailings a day to Lismore. Already alongside loading is the Inner Isles vessel *Lochearn*. Interestingly, she had replaced *Lochmor* on the service. *Lochearn* was due to leave Oban at 0600 on Mondays, Wednesdays and Fridays and was due back around 1500 on Tuesdays, Thursdays and Saturdays. On the inward passage she normally left Lochboisdale around 2000 the previous evening and Castlebay at midnight. The domed pier building had only just been erected in 1927, with the MacBrayne offices on one side, and a marshalling shed on the other.

***Princess Louise* (1898) in Oban Bay September 1935.** This tidy little vessel was built for a private operator, Alexander Paterson of Oban and remained in his ownership until being taken over by MacBrayne in 1934. She had been primarily engaged in providing short cruises for Paterson, often to the smaller, out of the way destinations that MacBrayne did not serve. On being taken over by MacBrayne she continued doing this but also spent some time at Inverness providing a day cruise from there to Fort Augustus. Another lucrative source of employment was livestock carrying which MacBrayne continued. To demonstrate the point, we can see two horses standing on the foredeck below the bridge. She was evidently a relaxed vessel in operation as is demonstrated by the two passengers standing on the bridge in front of the helmsman!

Princess Louise* at Oban 4th September 1935.** *Princess Louise* slowly steams across Oban Bay heading for the Railway Pier. Her cargo on this occasion is composed solely of sheep and they are packed in tight all the way from the bow to the stern with one of her crew seemingly stuck right in the middle of them. The carriage of livestock was a very lucrative business for MacBrayne and frequently involved vessels being seconded in the autumn to do nothing else. The various crofters and estates raised the beasts during the summer then sent them either to market to be sold or else to pastures in the North East of Scotland where the grazing was more plentiful in winter. Often, MacBrayne vessels would carry more sheep, cattle, horses and pigs than they would passengers! Just over her bridge can be seen ***Lochfyne lying at the top of the pier.

King George V* alongside the Railway Pier, Oban 2nd August 1936.** As it is a Sunday, ***King George V is lying out of service at the Railway Pier in her first season in MacBrayne colours. She was fitted with two additional lifeboats on the after deck: these were transferred from ***Columba*** and had originated in the ***Scout***. Although Williamson-Buchanan were jointly taken over by MacBrayne and the LM&SR the plan was initially that of MacBrayne who wanted to get their hands on ***King George V*** and ***Queen Alexandra*** as ready made replacements for the venerable duo of ***Columba*** and ***Iona***. The takeover officially took place in October 1935 and both steamers had their funnels quickly painted red. Unlike the Glasgow vessels the crews did not transfer with the vessels and MacBrayne personnel manned them both. The ***George*** was put on the Staffa and Iona service where she quickly became a great favourite. Oban folk only considered that summer had started when the ***George*** first appeared at the pier. In the background can be seen the clock tower of the railway station which only actually had three clocks, the fourth face being blank.

Lochfyne* (1931) at anchor off Iona 3rd August 1931.** The new owners of the MacBrayne fleet caused the winds of change to blow on the West Coast and in the case of ***Lochfyne, they were positively howling! She was the first British ship to be fitted with diesel electric propulsion whereby the propellers were driven by direct-coupled electric motors which were powered by diesel engines, a system which engendered enormous public and professional interest. She was designed to cruise to Staffa and Iona from Oban in summer and then transfer to the Tarbert and Ardrishaig service in winter. She was a very economical vessel but was cursed by an excess of noise and vibration. On the Iona cruise the vessel anchored in the Sound and her passengers were ferried ashore to the island. In the photograph we can see the open ferry door with steps fitted that passengers used to transfer to the smaller vessels. Loading and unloading took time and on busy days it was a nightmare for her purser to ensure that passengers returned at their allotted time. Note also the seaman standing on her stern fender cleaning the name! In the background is Fionnphort on the Ross of Mull.

Lochmor* (1930) and *Fusilier* (1888) at Mallaig 25th May 1931.** The old and the new meet at Mallaig in 1932. The old came in the form of ***Fusilier which was delivered in 1888 and had a varied career with the Company which ended with her being the Portree Mail vessel. ***Lochmor*** was one of a pair of twins delivered in 1930 to take up the sailings from Oban, Mallaig and Kyle of Lochalsh to the Inner and Outer Hebrides. The new vessels were certainly not pretty and in some aspects were ugly but they were imposing and they provided much better facilities for passengers than the ancient vessels they replaced. This was particularly true of the Third Class accommodation which on the older ships was described as being not fit for sheep. Whether that was accurate Third Class on the new vessels was comfortable and contained usable toilets!

Lochnevis* (1934) arriving at Mallaig September 1934.** This shot shows ***Lochnevis arriving at her southern terminal of Mallaig in her first season. She brought a whole new concept of comfort to the service and became instantly popular with travellers and islanders alike. Before the Second World War the Portree route was the principal route on and off Skye and during the high season was a busy route for passenger traffic. However, for most of the year, passenger numbers were low but her diesel electric propulsion system greatly reduced the running costs of the service compared to the coal fired ***Glencoe*** and ***Fusilier***. MacBrayne made a point of extolling the importance of the breakfasts sold on board their vessels and it was widely believed that the best breakfasts in the fleet were those served on board ***Lochnevis***. In a slower paced age there was plenty of time to savour the delights of a meal served by an immaculately dressed steward at your table. Sadly, such scenes are now but a memory! The canvas screen was only put in place behind the small lounge when ***Lochnevis*** was operating north of Oban.

Lochiel **(1906) at Kyle of Lochalsh with** ***Lochness*** **(1929) September 1934.** Berthed on the south side of Kyle of Lochalsh railway pier we see the cargo vessel *Lochiel* at rest. She was awarded to MacBrayne as a replacement for the previous *Lochiel* which had been lost in the Great War and entered the fleet in 1919. She was sometimes employed on the Stornoway cargo service but in the autumn could usually be found undertaking special livestock sailings to bring thousands of animals in from the islands either to be wintered in Easter Ross or to be slaughtered in the lowlands and this would account for her presence at Kyle. At the other side of the pier lies the Stornoway vessel *Lochness* loading cargo for Lewis. Large containers are waiting on the pier to be slung aboard by Kyle's large steam crane which is seen at her bow. The Kyle railway line provided the connection from Kyle to Inverness.

Lochness **(1929) leaving Kyle of Lochalsh September 1934.** In 1928 MacBrayne was taken over by a combination of Coast Lines and the LM&SR and they were instructed to build four new vessels, the first of which was *Lochness* which was for the Stornoway service. An imposing vessel, *Lochness* was the last steamship to be built for MacBrayne and was a vast improvement on what had gone before, providing new standards of comfort, particularly for Third Class passengers. She sailed every evening from Stornoway at 2345 and made for Applecross and then on to Kyle and Mallaig. Arriving at the latter around 0700 she discharged and loaded cargo then sailed light to Kyle to load cargo before leaving in mid afternoon for Applecross and Stornoway. Passengers for her from Mallaig were carried by the Portree steamer then changed to *Lochness* at Kyle. This allowed her ample time to load the vast mounds of cargo waiting at Kyle, including wool for the Harris Tweed industry. During the week she had barely 24 hours rest, which of course was on Sundays.

***Lochness* (1929) at Kyle 23 May 1931.** Taken from the grounds of the Lochalsh Hotel, this photograph provides an excellent view of the Stornoway vessel. Although many purists derided her for not being as handsome as some of her predecessors she was an extremely successful vessel which proved instantly popular with the Lewis public. Capable of a speed of 14 knots she speeded up the journey time across the Minch and was an excellent vessel in heavy seas. The company proudly boasted that the mails always got through and it is thought that she never missed a crossing despite what the weather could throw at her. That being said, the Minch definitely remained a place not for the fainthearted, or stomached, in gale conditions!

Glencoe* (1846) arriving at Portree 23rd May 1931.** At around 1730 *Glencoe* steams into her base, Portree, for the last time. Waiting for her there was ***Fusilier which had been chosen by MacBraynes to replace her on the Portree service. Beginning in 1846 sailing from Glasgow to Lochalsh and Stornoway, ***Glencoe*** was employed on a variety of routes which ranged from Glasgow to Inveraray with cargo, Oban to Gairloch, West Loch Tarbert to Islay and the Portree service. Not content with that, she sailed on charter to the CSP on the Clyde for a period during the Great War. She was refitted as a saloon steamer in 1875 and had several new boilers but retained her original engines throughout her life. By 1931 she was a museum piece and it is difficult to comprehend the contrasts between her and the 1930s twins ***Lochearn*** and ***Lochmor***. When she was exhibited alongside ***Lochfyne*** at Glasgow in 1931 more attention was probably lavished on her than on the new vessel! Her passing was a source of great regret to many in the Highlands and Islands.

Glencoe (1846) alongside *Fusilier* at Portree 24th May 1931. As she lies alongside *Fusilier* at Portree we can have a detailed look at the design of the old vessel which displayed what would have been considered normal for a mid Victorian vessel. Thus the engine room telegraph can be found on the top of the paddle box while the steering wheel is behind the housing for the steeple engine just forward of the funnel. She did not possess a navigating bridge as such and the helmsman stood on a platform peering over the housing while the officer of the watch could only see the way forward by standing on top of the paddle. Conditions on board for the passengers were decidedly dated and one can only imagine what the living conditions of her crew were. After being exhibited with *Lochfyne* the old vessel was broken up; sadly, the concept of preservation was unknown at the time.

On board *Glencoe* (1846) at Portree May 1931. The West Coast of Scotland has been served by several vessels with amazingly long careers and possibly the most venerable was *Glencoe* which lasted in service from 1846 until 1931. In her case, she was employed all year round on routes which required the vessel to face the full rigours of a West Coast winter. By the time of her demise she was a museum piece with the original steeple engine fitted when new and with fixtures and fittings from a bygone age. One of these was the carving of a golden eagle, shown here, which was placed beside the entrance to her Dining Saloon at the aft end of the vessel. As with most vessels of her time various embellishments such as carvings were included which provided a type of decoration that was unheard of on later vessels. She was not the only vessel so adorned, the Loch Ness paddler *Glengarry* had a similar carving on board. That *Glencoe* sailed for eighty five years is a glowing testimonial to Clyde built vessels of the period. Beyond the tricky approaches to Portree Bay is the faint outline of the island of Raasay.

Glencoe (1846) and *Fusilier* (1888) at Portree 23rd May 1931. The old and the new Skye vessels spend Sunday together lying at Portree. Having arrived for the last time the previous day, *Glencoe* takes her ease before sailing to the Clyde at the end of her career the following day. Inside her lies *Fusilier* ready to take up the service on Monday morning. While *Fusilier* brought a whole new concept of comfort to the route she was in a way a strange choice to be the Skye Mail vessel as she was completely devoid of cargo handling gear which meant that her crew had the pleasure of manhandling all cargo down a gangway or a cargo chute, no joke at low tide at Kyle, despite the cattle ramp on the pier. Several of the latter's crew are in civilian clothes; Sunday was most certainly not a day of work on board a MacBrayne vessel! Many would use the opportunity to go to a religious service ashore. *Fusilier* was only used on the route in the summer and for the rest of the year it was entrusted to *Plover*.

Glencoe (1846) and *Fusilier* (1888) alongside at Portree 24th May 1931. After a varied career that saw her on a variety of routes from Stornoway in the north to Loch Fyne in the south, *Glencoe* took over the Portree service after the Great War and remained on it until her withdrawal in 1931. Based at Portree the vessel made a daily sailing, Sundays excepted, from Portree and Raasay to Kyle of Lochalsh and Mallaig, with calls at or off, Broadford, Glenelg and Armadale. As well as providing the main passenger access to Skye, the route also carried a variety of goods and livestock. At Kyle connection was made to the LM&SR route to Inverness and the south while at Mallaig she connected with L&NER trains to Fort William and Glasgow via the West Highland line. She is photographed at Portree alongside the vessel destined to replace her, *Fusilier*. Note also the collection of fishing smacks berthed outside her.

Lochbroom (1871) arriving at Portree September 1934, with *Lochiel* departing behind. From the formation of the new company in 1928 the MacBrayne fleet entered into a process of fleet renewal. Therefore, it seems unusual that in 1931 they purchased a 60 year old vessel to replace the famous ***Claymore*** which was only 50 years old. ***City of London*** had spent her life sailing between Aberdeen and London but she entered the MacBrayne fleet in 1931 and was renamed ***Lochbroom***. She was utilised on the West Coast cargo and passenger service which sailed from Glasgow every 10 days and called at a variety of ports as far north as Lochinver. The whole sailing was advertised as a cruise and quickly became very successful, so successful in fact that she was replaced in 1937 by the larger ***Lochgarry***, also bought second hand but in her case only a youth with 39 years service with Laird Line! Sadly, she didn't survive the war and the cruise was never revived after the war.

Lochnevis (1934) arriving at Portree September 1934. Just after five o'clock every weekday ***Lochnevis*** appeared around the headland at the entrance to the natural harbour beside which Portree was situated. She normally left Portree around 0745 in the morning on her way south and reached Mallaig just after midday. After a very brief turn round she was away again on the northbound sailing. Cargo for Raasay and Skye was loaded at both Mallaig and Kyle and on the way north she also carried passengers for Stornoway who subsequently changed to ***Lochness*** at Kyle. On certain days she stopped off Glenelg where a ferry came out to her and the ferry door, with lowered fender, can be seen on the port side amidships. Lying off the pier is a steam dredger which would have been carrying out dredging at Portree's pier. At very low tides ***Lochnevis*** could be just afloat and no more, so periodic dredging of her berth was a necessity.

Lochnevis* (1934) arriving at Portree September 1934.** The use of ***Fusilier on the Skye route was a temporary situation as, in 1934, the route was provided with a brand new vessel. This was ***Lochnevis*** which followed ***Lochfyne*** in being a diesel electric vessel. However her engine space was redesigned from that of the earlier vessel to eliminate much of the excess noise and vibration that the former suffered greatly from. As well as excellent passenger accommodation for two classes she was also provided with a cargo hold and cargo handling equipment. As well as the sailing to Kyle and Mallaig she also indulged in evening cruises from Portree to such spots as Loch Torridon and Gairloch. During the summer she also provided the weekly cruise from Mallaig to Loch Scavaig. The good people of Skye must have rubbed their eyes at the procession of vessels they received in a matter of three years and, compared to ***Glencoe***, ***Lochnevis*** must have appeared like something from a different planet.

Gondolier* (1866) in the Caledonian Canal July 1929.** The original Royal Route was a fascinating journey which commenced at Glasgow where passengers boarded ***Columba to sail to Ardrishaig which was reached at lunchtime. They then boarded ***Linnet*** to sail to Crinan and then ***Chevalier*** which sailed on to Oban, Fort William and Banavie at the southern end of the Caledonian Canal. The last link in the chain was on ***Gondolier*** which took them the length of the Caledonian Canal to Inverness. Thus passengers sailed on four different but fascinating vessels. Gradually over the years the vessels changed and the portion on the Crinan Canal was replaced by a more prosaic bus from Ardrishaig to Oban but ***Gondolier*** soldiered on until the beginning of the Second World War. Throughout its existence the MacBrayne organisation were masters of advertising and such routes opened up the Highlands and Islands to tourist traffic.

Gondolier* (1866) approaching Temple Pier, Loch Ness, July 1929.** In this evocative photograph we can discern the majestic *Gondolier* gliding into one of her Loch Ness calling points with a good load of passengers on board. To lovers of symbols of the earlier days of steam the MacBrayne fleet at the time was a copious treasure trove. With ***Gondolier (1866), ***Iona*** (1864), ***Columba*** (1878) and ***Glencoe*** (1846) one could almost think that they were still in mid Victorian times. However, while the fleet may have had enthusiasts of Victoriana drooling it was an expensive anachronism which needed urgent modernisation. This proved to be beyond the capabilities of the original owners with the result that the company was taken over by the LM&SR and Coast Lines in 1928. At the moment this photograph was taken the winds of change were just beginning to blow up.

Gondolier* (1866) at Inverness August 1933. *Gondolier was based at Inverness and sailed down the Canal to Banavie on Mondays, Wednesdays and Fridays and returned on Tuesdays, Thursdays and Saturdays. On the way she called at several stopping points such as Fort Augustus and, when she was navigating through a lock, passengers could go ashore and walk along the Canal. MacBrayne kept vessels in service for an amazing length of time and ***Gondolier*** was 71 years old when she finished. She was in the old tradition very ornately decorated but her accommodation was kept very modern. Unusually her fore saloon was the width of the vessel while her after saloon had alleyways round it. Her bow was of unusual shape, being designed to help "nudge" lock gates open. Note the change of funnel and forward saloon from the image on the previous page. In 1935 new saloons with larger windows were fitted and in 1936 a deckhouse was added. She had a sad end in 1939 when she was stripped of saloons and machinery with the hull then being towed to Scapa Flow where it was sunk to block a channel. Even in death she served her country.

***Juno* (1898) being broken up at Alloa Shipbreakers Ltd 14th February 1932.** The mighty *Juno* spent virtually all her peacetime career providing cruises out of Ayr, Troon and Ardrossan, the only exception being in 1919 when she was based upriver. Her programme was extremely varied and took her round the firth from Lochgoilhead and Garelochhead in the north to Stranraer in the south. However, the operating restrictions imposed on the G&SW in 1891 prohibited her cruising to Loch Fyne, the west side of Arran and Kintyre. She became an exceedingly popular vessel with the travelling public and thus the decision to withdraw her after the 1931 season initially proved to be very unpopular with her passengers. Sadly she carried the G&SW "curse" of high running costs and heavy maintenance bills. She was sold in early 1932 to an Alloa scrap metal dealer and left Greenock's Albert Harbour on 6th February for her final destination. On arrival she was beached but by the date of the shot little had been done to her externally. On her left also awaiting scrap is one of the Alloa steam ferries.

***Fair Maid* (1888) lying at Granton 22nd February 1936.** This fascinating vessel was built for Campbell's Glasgow to Kilmun service but very quickly passed to the nascent CSP in 1889. She had a successful career with them, serving principally the Holy Loch ports until being sold to Captain Cameron for sailings out of Glasgow. After the Great War she passed to Williamson and was renamed *Isle of Skye*. She found employment on their basic sailings from Glasgow to Rothesay until being withdrawn in 1927. She wasn't finished yet however because she was bought by the Grangemouth & Forth Towing Co. and taken round to the Firth of Forth to provide pleasure sailings and undertake tender work. She earned some useful revenue in the winter by being chartered by the L&NER to relieve on their Granton to Burntisland service to allow their vessel *William Muir* off for annual overhaul. Just to complete her eventful life she spent the Second World War as a tender on the Clyde under the management of the CSP and even fitted in a week sailing out of Craigendoran for the L&NER.

Fair Maid **(1888) on passage 22nd February 1936.** In the ordinary scheme of things a summer cruise vessel would spend a large part of the year laid up for want of business. However, ***Fair Maid*** found some employment sailing between Granton and Burntisland for the L&NER. This service was seen as the premier service across the Forth and was popular among Fife residents as a quick way to get to Edinburgh for work or recreation. Once at Granton buses and trams left frequently for the city. This shot gives an interesting idea what it would have been like to sail on a Victorian paddler. She had relatively large paddles and this is illustrated by the height the landing platform was above the deck. In the foreground can be seen a pipe from the coal stove in the saloon while the galley funnel is smoking away happily on the port sponson. There is also the bicycle stored behind the lifejacket locker!

Fair Maid **(1888) at Burntisland 22nd February 1936.** Having previously observed her at Granton we can now look at ***Fair Maid*** alongside at the Fife side of the Forth at Burntisland. Having carried out a sailing to Burntisland she is now waiting to undertake a sailing back across the river to the Lothian side. Given the complete lack of activity and the vigorous trail of smoke emerging from the galley funnel we can deduce that it is a crew meal break. We can see that the old vessel has the somewhat battered appearance of a cruise vessel out of season. Various streaks of rust can be seen on her sponson housing with more around the beading of the after saloon. Her funnel is somewhat dirty and her name has almost disappeared on the paddle box. No doubt on completion of the charter she would be heading for a local ship repair yard to begin her annual overhaul.

William Muir* (1879) arriving at Granton 19th March 1932.** Having completed another crossing of the Forth ***William Muir is sweeping round to berth at the East Pier where the ferry slipway was located. Also berthed just ahead of and outside the slipway is a vessel of the Northern Lighthouse Board; their vessels were taxed with the duty of supplying and maintaining the lighthouses and navigational aids around the Scottish coast and as far south as the Isle of Man. With their distinctive yellow funnels they were a familiar sight berthed at Granton, Oban and Stromness in Orkney. On this particular crossing ***William Muir*** is not exactly loaded with traffic!

William Muir* (1879) berthed at Granton 19th March 1932.** The Granton to Burntisland ferry service was operated by the L&NER and was seen by them as being more important than that between North and South Queensferry. It was operated by the venerable paddler ***William Muir which had been built in 1879. Originally she had two funnels but in 1910 she was rendered into the condition photographed. She was unusual in that she had an ornate whaleback fo'castle. Her funnel was painted in the traditional NB/L&NER red and black with a white band. She is berthed at the ferry slipway on the Edinburgh side of Granton harbour awaiting her next crossing. Although she did not provide any sort of cruising each round trip was advertised as a non-landing sailing with a fare that was slightly less than the ordinary return. It is interesting to note that Captain Donald Crawford, a well-known master on the Clyde commanded ***William Muir*** for a period just before and after the Second World War.

BL Nairn crossing the Tay 14th September 1932. Compared to the thoroughbreds in service on the Clyde this vessel looks decidedly unusual but she was an important part of Scotland's transport system. She operated on the service across the Tay from the Fife side to Dundee and carried both vehicles and passengers. Fitted with compound diagonal disconnecting engines which allowed the paddle wheels to be used independently of each other she was able to cross in 10 to 20 minutes depending on the tide. Despite being joined by more modern vessels these were not as reliable as she was and **BL Nairn** remained in daily use up until the service closed on 18th June 1966 upon the opening of the Tay Road Bridge. Popularly known as the Fifies, the ferries before the war indulged in some short cruising as well as the ferry crossing but the continuous growth in vehicle traffic stopped this practice after the conflict. On completion of the bridge, she was scrapped in Blyth. On her left can just be discerned the Tay Railway Bridge.

The popular types of machinery and the decades in which they were common are listed in James Williamson's magisterial book – *The Clyde Passenger Steamer – Its Rise and Progress during the Nineteenth Century*.

During the 1840s the type of engine for each ship is listed and they are predominantly steeple. In the 1850s the steeple engine remained the popular choice but there were also a few oscillating engines. During the 1860s the oscillating engine overtook the steeple engine in popularity until 1868 when the single diagonal engine made an appearance. In the 1870s decade, the single and double diagonal engine became the engine of choice for the majority of ship owners and this continued through the 1880s until 1889 when the CSP commissioned Caledonia which although a single crank engine was driven by a two cylinder, compound, tandem engine.

From 1890 onwards the development of the Clyde passenger steamer was driven by the two powerful Scottish railway companies – The Caledonian Railway Company through their wholly owned subsidiary the Caledonian Steam Packet Company (CSP) and the Glasgow and South Western Railway Company (G&SWR). From the 1889 *Caledonia* forward the machinery of all paddlers built up until 1931 was two cylinder compound with either a single crank but more commonly twin crank. John Williamson followed the twin crank, compound path probably helped by the earnings of his two turbine steamers but the Buchanan Brothers stuck with the single diagonal when they built *Isle of Arran* in 1892 and *Eagle III* in 1910: the single diagonal engine by A. & J. Inglis being the last to be built on Clydeside.

STEAM ENGINES
The Steeple Engine
This type of engine was the invention of David Napier and had the cylinder located in the bottom of the ship with the piston driving vertically upwards with its crosshead, to which the connecting rod was connected, sliding in two entablatures that resembled a church steeple. This type of engine was unique as it had four piston rods rather than the customary single rod in the centre of the piston. The four rods were necessary to clear the crank shaft and connecting rod.

This engine benefitted from being smooth running with no tiresome forward thrust motion but, despite the cylinder being in the bottom, the steeple part was both extensive and heavy and the effect of its high centre of gravity probably gave rise to complaints about the ship's behaviour in a seaway. Another drawback was that by their design they were not suited to fitting Stephenson's link motion to aid reversing which had to be done by disconnecting the single eccentric valve gear with the engineer operating the slide valve by hand while trying to reverse the direction of the engine without stalling and the piston dropping to the bottom of the cylinder. When this happened it was all engine room hands tailing on to a permanently fitted, long pinch bar until they managed to lever the piston over bottom dead centre and allowed steam to act on the underside of the piston. Like all paddle steamers if the vessel had any forward motion the effect of the paddle floats would cause the engine to continue to be turned in the original direction with the engineer desperately trying to "catch" the reverse direction by working the slide valve by hand.

The Oscillating Engine
This engine, usually twin cylinder, was more expensive to manufacture than the steeple type but it had positive advantages in that it was compact, had a low centre of gravity with fewer moving parts and could be fitted with Stephenson's link motion for ease of reversing. It was also a very smooth running engine but it had a disadvantage in that the cylinders oscillated on a hollow bearing, or trunnion, on each side through which the boiler and exhaust steam entered and left the cylinders. Keeping the trunnions steam tight was the main disadvantage of this type of engine and it restricted the level of the boiler steam pressure that the engine could economically accept. In other words with a fixed steam pressure and revolutions fixed by the circumference of the paddle wheel, the only means of getting more power was to increase the bore and stroke of the cylinders. In PS *Columba*'s case she required two cylinders each of 53 inches diameter and 66 inches stroke to achieve her designed speed although her great length also contributed to achieving this speed.

The Single Diagonal or Single Expansion Engine
This was the steam engine in its most basic form and could be described as a horizontal factory engine placed in a ship with its cylinder near the bottom of the ship and its crankshaft connected to the paddle wheel shaft giving a sloping, or diagonal arrangement. The engine was quite unsophisticated in that the valve gear was only automatically able to drive the engine when going ahead and when it came to having to reverse or manoeuvre the engine, the gear had to be disconnected and the valve gear then operated manually by the engineer. From various published reports it was often a hazardous experience for both the engine and the engineer until he had fully mastered the technique. Both the CSP and the NBSP fitted steam valve gear actuators on the single crank engines built for them in the last decade of the 19th Century. They eased the physical effort for the engineer but he had still to watch his timing judgement!

Like the oscillating engine, the cylinder dimensions were determined by the boiler steam pressure and as the steam pressure had to expand down to a vacuum with a corresponding increase in steam volume this type of

Single Diagonal Engine of *Talisman* (1896) photographed in 1933.

engine required both a long stroke and a large cylinder volume. Because of the expansion limitation there was a restriction on the maximum boiler pressure that could be used and in 1889 this was neatly solved on *Caledonia* by Rankin & Blackmore when they introduced double expansion by fitting a second cylinder for this purpose. The first compound engine built for Clyde paddle steamer service!

With the exception of the CSP's three, new-build, single crank engines, the engine rooms of the other single crank engined ships were quite lacking in independently driven auxiliary machinery with the air pump, a boiler feed pump and the condenser cooling water circulating pump all driven by rocker arms from the main engine. There was no steam driven electric generator or forced draft fan but there would be an independent boiler feed pump and a single steam driven bilge, fire and general service pump.

The Two Crank Compound or Double Expansion Engine

In parallel with the building of the 1889 *Caledonia*, the CSP also built two, double crank compound engined ships, *Galatea* and *Duchess of Hamilton* and a two crank triple expansion engined *Marchioness of Lorne*. These were all ships with independently driven engine room auxiliaries and all were fitted with forced draft that had to have enclosed stokeholds and a steam driven fan to maintain the air pressure. To utilise waste heat, they were also fitted with feed heaters that raised the temperature of the water being returned from the condenser to the boiler giving a reduction in fuel consumption.

When the G&SWR were given parliamentary authority to operate Clyde passenger steamers, they embarked on a major shipbuilding programme and all their paddle steamers were fitted with twin crank compound engines.

The Twin Crank Triple Expansion Engine

Marchioness of Lorne of 1891 is usually credited with being fitted with the first triple expansion engine but she was really a two crank double compound engine as she had two high pressure cylinders that discharged into the intermediate and low pressure cylinders. She was fitted with this type of engine in the hope that on the longer winter runs between Brodick and Ardrossan, she would show a significant benefit in thermal efficiency with consequent reduced fuel consumption. I don't think this could have been so as Williamson mentions when speaking of the triple expansion engine that there are problems with cylinder condensation; probably there was no steam jacketing of the cylinders on the *Lorne*'s engines.

The Three Crank Triple Expansion Engine

The first proper "three legged steamer" was *Jeanie Deans* of 1931 built for the L&NER with no similar ship built for them until *Waverley* entered service in 1947. Both of these ships had conventional engines fitted with Stephenson's valve gear and had the latest and most up to date auxiliary machinery in their engine rooms with the possible exception of the steam turbine driven generating sets fitted to the CSP (LM&S) paddlers built in the 1930s. Unlike the CSP, the L&NER made an excursion into diesel-electric propulsion when they commissioned *Talisman* in 1935.

The CSP paddle steamers that were built in the 1930s were all fitted with three cylinder triple expansion engines but all had single eccentric valve gear. The Fairfield built ships had that company's patent valve gear based on

*Compound Diagonal Engine of **Waverley** (1899) photographed in 1932.*

either the Joy or Bremme valve gear and **Caledonia** had Denny-Brock valve gear which gave a very sharp steam cut-off.

BOILERS
The early boilers which were very thermally inefficient and only able to raise steam at a very low pressure are not relevant to these notes. The types of boiler considered are:

The Haystack Boiler
This type of boiler which is of the water tube type, gets its name from its size and shape. It is light in weight, has a large grate area that gives rapid steaming and during the 50 years that it held sway its working pressure was gradually increased due to improved boiler design; the development of wrought iron with better strength characteristics; the introduction of more efficient boiler making plant and equipment; and lastly, the gradual change of material from wrought iron to mild steel from 1880 onwards

In the 1850s the steeple engine and the haystack boiler were favourite but by the 1860s both the diagonal engine and the oscillating engine were equally popular with the haystack working at 40 psi. By the 1870s and through the 1880s the combination was the diagonal engine with haystack boiler working at 50 psi.

In 1896 A. & J. Inglis developed a haystack boiler for Talisman working at 65psi and in 1899, when sister ship **Kenilworth** was built, it was recognised that the single engine had reached its peak and as the NBSP's next ship had to be faster and therefore more powerful to compete with the opposition, it was decided to fit a two crank compound diagonal engine. To power this engine Inglis developed a haystack boiler that worked at 110 psi which allowed the NBSP to have its first and very successful two crank compound paddle engine fitted in 1899 to **Waverley**. The Clyde owners never considered fitting forced draft to the haystack boiler hence the tall funnel and the group of four ventilators around its base. I believe P. & A. Campbell did fit a forced draft haystack boiler to two of their "crack" paddlers.

Waverley's compound engine was followed by **Lucy Ashton** and **Marmion** with each being fitted with a compound engine and haystack boiler. I think it can be taken that it was the 1902 compound engine fitted to **Lucy Ashton** that ensured her longevity as she was a fuel efficient winter boat when traffic level was low.

The Navy Boiler
The Navy Boiler is technically a locomotive type of boiler which is contained in a cylindrical shell and has one or more furnaces at the front, or firing, end of the boiler, a combustion chamber at mid-length and a smokebox at the back end. There is a large number of horizontal fire tubes from the combustion chamber to the smokebox through which the product of combustion gasses pass and so heat the boiler water and raise steam.

The adjective Navy derives from the boilers being initially designed for the Royal Navy's fast torpedo boats and torpedo boat destroyers that were developed from the 1880s and which required a relatively light weight and compact boiler to provide steam for their very high revolution triple expansion engines.

The Navy's experience with this type of boiler was not a happy one as, when fitted with forced draft, they had endless trouble with leaking tubeplates caused by excessive use of forced draft. James Williamson had similar problems initially with **Caledonia** but, despite these early problems, the CSP persevered and all new construction, with the exception of **Duchess of Rothesay** and **Duchess of Argyll**, were fitted with Navy Boilers.

When in 1934 the LMS built the new **Mercury** and **Caledonia** they were fitted with Navy Boilers thus continuing the CSP's paddler tradition.

On the other hand, the Royal Navy's solution was to look to industry for a long term solution and the Yarrow 3-drum Water Tube boiler was born; as was a somewhat similar water tube boiler developed by Thornycroft of Southampton.

This type of boiler was not fitted in any Clyde steamer until 1926 when it was installed in **King George V** as part of the high pressure turbine experiment but with unfortunate results: but that is another story.

The Single Ended Return Tube or Scotch Boiler

The Scotch boiler is a cylindrical boiler of the fire tube type and, in association with the triple expansion engine, was the machinery of choice for the world's merchant cargo fleet for the best part of 60 years.

The boiler was not dissimilar in external appearance to the Navy type but internally was quite different. The boiler had circular corrugated furnaces ranging from a single one in a small diameter boiler up to four in a larger diameter one. The furnace terminated in a combustion chamber at the back end of the boiler and from this chamber there was a large number of horizontal fire tubes that returned from the combustion chamber through the boiler to the smokebox/funnel uptake at the boiler front. Like the Navy boiler it was through the fire tubes that the product of combustion gasses passed and heated the boiler water and so raised steam.

I assume the "Scotch" name must have to do with its development having taken place on Clydeside but its proper name of "return tube" derives from the reversed direction of the products of combustion from front to rear and back to the front again.

Apart from **Neptune** and **Mercury** which were sister ships of the Bristol Channel paddler **Lorna Doone**, all the G&SWR's paddle steamers were fitted with Return Tube Marine Boilers working under forced draught in association with compound diagonal engines.

The Double Ended Return Tube or Scotch Boiler

This type of boiler was, in effect, two single ended return tube boilers fitted back to back in a common boiler shell with a short separation between the two combustion chambers. Depending upon the layout of the ship the products of combustion could either be combined into a single funnel or two separate ones as in **Juno** and **Jupiter** of 1937 and **Waverley** as completed in 1947.

CONDENSERS
Jet Type

This type of condenser was the type invented by James Watt on his Sunday walk on Glasgow Green when he realised that there would be a huge gain in thermal efficiency of the steam engine if the steam was condensed in a vessel separate from the steam cylinder of the engine. Up until this point the spent steam in the cylinder was condensed by introducing a spray of cold water that had the desired effect but had the undesired effect of chilling the cylinder that had to be warmed again by the introduction of the steam at the next stroke of the engine; thoroughly inefficient and causing increased fuel consumption. Watt's invention solved this problem and by also insulating the cylinder of the engine, even with timber, the operating efficiency was much increased.

When applied to land based engines or ships operating in inland waters where there is a plentiful supply of fresh cooling water this type of condenser is quite acceptable as **Sir Walter Scott** has amply demonstrated for 120 years on Loch Katrine. However, when the Jet Condenser was applied to sea-going ships the use of salt water for condensing the exhaust steam had a marked effect on the boiler as the various constituents in sea water when pumped back into the boiler as part of the condensed feed water, caused a build up of scale on the internal surfaces of the boiler which reduced the transfer of heat from the fire tubes to the water and where the build up became excessive and was not attended to, there was the danger of overheating of the tube causing it to fail and disable the boiler.

Surface Condensing Type

This type of condenser started to be introduced in the mid 1870s and quickly became the standard for all types of marine steam engines. Like the Jet type it was a vessel separate from the engine but, unlike the Jet type, the condensate and the salt cooling water never met each other and, as a result, there was no contamination of the condensed feed water being returned to the boiler.

The principle of the surface condenser is very simple in that the exhaust steam from the engine passes through a bank of small bore tubes which are surrounded by a continuous flow of pumped sea water. The cool sea water causes the steam to condense and it is discharged from the condenser into the hot well tank. From the hot well tank this water is returned to the boiler as feed water by the boiler feed pump and as it is pure condensed water, there is no introduction of harmful sea water constituents and no build up of harmful scale.

Ian Ramsay, who wrote this Appendix, was well respected in the Clyde shipbuilding industry, having started his career as an apprentice at the A. & J. Inglis yard, and, following National Service, he returned there as General Manager until the yard closed in 1963. Thereafter he turned his skills to warship building at Yarrows, where he rose to the position of Shipbuilding Director, before joining Sir J. H. Biles, where he developed a team specialising in providing technical support for the Royal Navy. After retirement in 1997 he became Safety Director of the current **Waverley** and sadly passed away in May 2021.

APPENDIX 2 - STEAMER OWNERSHIP

During the period covered by this book the vessels operating on the Clyde were owned by six different operating companies. The biggest fleets were those of the railway companies, the London, Midland and Scottish Railway Company and the London and North Eastern Railway Company. Other owners were Williamson-Buchanan Steamers, David MacBrayne, the impressively named Glasgow and Campbeltown Joint Stock Steam Packet Company and Clyde Cargo Steamers.

London, Midland and Scottish Railway

Set up by the Grouping of 1923 the LM&SR took over the assets of the Caledonian Railway and the Glasgow and South Western Railway. The Caledonian and its predecessors first made their entrance in 1841 when they opened a line from Glasgow to Greenock (Cathcart Street) and starteding operating services from Customhouse Quay, Greenock to the coast by arranging for a private owner to connect with their trains. For a short time they tried operating vessels themselves but soon gave up and went back to relying on private owners. In 1865 they reached the coast at Wemyss Bay and again tried to operate their own vessels but again quickly gave that up in favour of cooperating with private owners. There the matter rested until 1869 when the Glasgow and South Western opened a terminal at Greenock (Albert Harbour). They also happily arranged for private owners to provide the steamer connections but had the great advantage of having their station virtually beside the vessels while passengers on the Caley Greenock line had to walk a distance from the station to the pier passing through a rather insalubrious area in the process. The convenience of the Albert Harbour arrangement meant that the South Western soon were carrying the lionne's share of traffic, much to the Caley's disgust.

To take them on the Caley eventually decided to extend the line from Greenock to Gourock where a new pier and station was to be erected. This proved to be an exceedingly expensive undertaking which involved digging a tunnel under Greenock's West End and the construction of a long pier and station on reclaimed land. By 1888 such was the progress of the work that the Caley started to make plans for a connecting steamer service by approaching the main steamboat owners and asking them to connect with trains at the new terminal. The response they got was judged to be totally inadequate given how much had been invested and led to the railway deciding to do it themselves. Thus, several new vessels were ordered, others were bought in and the company drew up a bid for Parliamentary approval for them to operate their own vessels. This horrified the private owners who immediately thought this would be a disaster for them and so they objected vigorously to Parliament mentioning the word dreaded by the Victorians – Monopoly. Parliament agreed and the Caley's Bill was thrown out.

Having started building up a fleet and then been banned from doing so the Caley reacted with a legal subterfuge. Several directors of the railway formed a nominally independent company, The Caledonian Steam Packet Company which assumed ownership of the vessels and entered into an agreement with the railway to operate services from Gourock. In 1890 they started operating the Wemyss Bay sailings and opened a new service from Ardrossan and Arran in competition with the South Western. At a stroke the Caley turned the tables on their rivals and became the predominant operator on the Clyde.

As well as the Albert Harbour line the Glasgow and South Western also ran lines to Fairlie and Ardrossan where private operators provided services to Millport and the east side of Arran. As a consequence of the Caley's actions the South Western faced disaster and needed to react fast while they still had any traffic left. They decided to emulate the Caley and ordered new vessels and bought in second hand ships and applied to Parliament for permission to operate them. They got precisely the same reaction from the private owners who immediately objected. However, given the Caley's shenanigans, there was sympathy for the South Western and they were given the permission required, with the proviso that they were not allowed to sail to Loch Fyne ports, the west side of Arran or to Kintyre. As a consequence of all this plotting a period of great and glorious, but totally uneconomic, competition revolutionised Clyde steamer services which continued until the Grouping although latterly both companies began to cooperate and share services.

Upon the Grouping the two fleets became one with, after a few years, a common colour scheme. However, for legal reasons, the former Caley vessels remained under the ownership of the Caledonian Steam Packet Company while the South Western vessels were directly owned by the LM&SR which led to the fleet having two houseflags. The LM&SR drew its custom from the South bank of the Clyde, Glasgow, Lanarkshire, Renfrewshire and Ayrshire and connections were also organised from Edinburgh (Princes Street) mostly by passengers changing trains at Glasgow (Central)

London and North Eastern Railway

Compared to the fun and games experienced on the South Bank, the development of services on the north side of the river was relatively straightforward. The North British Railway reached Helensburgh by 1865 and immediately began a steamer service to various points on the firth. The seemingly usual result for railways and the Clyde was a disaster and the service was quickly withdrawn. However, in 1869, they tried again in a much more modest way and soon built up a respectable amount of business. Over the next few years they gradually built up their fleet but their operation was faced with the major disadvantage that Helensburgh pier and station were far apart and passengers were faced with a long trek from one to an the other. However, in 1882, the situation was improved by the building of a new station and pier at Craigendoran, several miles east of Helensburgh. This enabled passengers to transfer from ship to train very quickly and easily.

The North British company were a very canny lot and decided that the building of expensive vessels was a silly idea and instead built a fleet of more modest vessels that weren't as luxurious as those of the Caley and the South Western but were much more economical to operate. As a result they had a healthier financial situation compared to their competitors. Their traffic was naturally drawn from the north side of the Clyde, including, Dumbarton, Clydebank, Glasgow and North Lanarkshire. Connections were also available from Edinburgh (Waverley) via Glasgow (Queen Street). However, they had the geographical disadvantage of Craigendoran being further away from the main resorts of Dunoon and Rothesay with corresponding longer journey times.

At the Grouping in 1923 the North British was absorbed into the new London and North Eastern Company. However, unlike their South Bank rivals, nothing really changed. The colour scheme continued as before although a new system wide houseflag was adopted. As the 1920's and 30's progressed the L&NER found itself being increasingly challenged and ultimately overtaken by the LM&SR with a consequent cutting of services and increasing talk among some shareholders that their steamer services should be given up.

Williamson-Buchanan Steamers

In 1853 the Captains Williamson and Buchanan were the principal owners of the steamer Eagle sailing out of Glasgow. However, in 1862, they went their own ways and began operating their own vessels. Buchanan principally operated sailings from Glasgow's Broomielaw, mostly to Dunoon, Rothesay and the Kyles and gradually began to build up a fleet and expand his services. Thus, in 1874, he also began operating a service from Ardrossan to Arran in conjunction with the G&SWR while in 1885 he took over the fleet of Keith and Campbell and soon was operating services throughout the Clyde including to the Gareloch ports, Cumbrae and the island of Arran. On the passing of the original Captain Buchanan the fleet was eventually reconstituted as a limited company in 1905. The arrival of the railway owned vessels and the malodorous state of the Clyde served to put a brake on services and by the Great War the fleet was smaller and principally engaged on the Rothesay trade.

Williamson meanwhile also began to slowly build up a fleet, again sailing out of Glasgow and produced the famous "Turkish" fleet of vessels, so called because of their names (Sultan, Sultana etc). He became the principal supplier of vessels to sail in connection with G&SWR steamers from Greenock and also started sailings from the Kyles of Bute to Glasgow. In 1892 he was succeeded by his son John but the company also suffered from the rise of railway vessels and retrenched. By the end of the 19thth century John was providing a service to Campbeltown from Fairlie for the G&SWR and this led to his involvement in the Turbine Syndicate which introduced the world's first commercially operated turbine steamer, King Edward, in 1901. Such was the success of this innovation that he introduced other turbine steamers and operated services to both Campbeltown and Inveraray. At the same time, he continued to operate the traditional services to Rothesay and the Kyles.

Both Williamson and Buchanan catered for working class passengers who were happy to put up with the state of the river because travelling as such was cheaper than using the railway services to the coast. This led to their vessels not being as grand as the Caley and South Western but both made a good living so doing. However they were badly affected by the Great War which greatly curtailed services although some income was made by chartering vessels to the railway companies whose fleets had been virtually denuded by the Admiralty. At the end of the War the two companies amalgamated and Williamson-Buchanan Steamers was borne. They continued to provide their usual services and made a good living but by the 1930's the owners saw the writing on the wall as regarded competition from the LM&SR fleet and decided to sell out to them and MacBrayne in 1935.

David MacBrayne Limited

From the beginnings of steam navigation on the Clyde vessels were owned by a bewildering assortment of owners but as the century moved on some owners took over others and gradually built up fleets. One such was the fleet of G. &and J. Burns who built up an empire encompassing vessels on the Clyde, the Western Isles and the Irish Sea. By the end of the 1840's they decided to consolidate their Irish Sea services and withdraw from the rest; they handed over their West Highland interests to one of their employees, David Hutcheson who gave his name to the enterprise and worked with his brother, Alexander. The Burns's insisted that their nephew, one David MacBrayne, should work with them with a view to taking over when Hutcheson retired. Hutcheson radically improved the services to such an extent that a monument to him was erected on the north end of Kerrera at the entrance to Oban Bay in recognition of the part he had played in the development of Oban as an important port for West Highland services.

David retired in 1876 and his brother two years later, after which the organisation became the legendary David MacBrayne Company. MacBrayne ran the company single handed until 1902 when his sons David Hope MacBrayne and Laurence MacBrayne became partners. After this he took a back seat while the sons ran the enterprise but, in 1906, David Hope took it over and turned it into a Private Limited Company.

All went well until after the Great War when the changed economic circumstances brought about by the conflict began to increase costs and reduce profits. The 1920's proved to be a most unfortunate time as no fewer than three vessels were lost, Sheila and Chevalier by grounding and Grenadier by fire. With an ageing fleet and diminishing returns the company was overwhelmed and announced in 1928 that it didn't intend applying to renew the mail contract. As no other organisation showed the slightest interest in taking over the government was placed in the position that it had to intervene to maintain the vital sea links to the islands. Thus, a new company was formed which was 50% owned by Coast Lines and 50% by the LM&SR. Now known as David MacBrayne (1928) Limited the new owners began a period of urgent modernisation and expansion. The numeral was dropped from the name in 1934.

Throughout its history the company reigned supreme in terms of passenger services but faced competition from others in the provision of cargo services.

Glasgow and Campbeltown Joint Stock Steam Packet Company

In 1826 a group of Campbeltown merchants and gentlemen gathered together in Campbeltown to review the provision of reliable steamboat services to the town. They expressed the collective view that the area was not enjoying the economic benefits of the new world of steamships and decided to remedy the situation by forming their own company. Thus, the magnificently named company came into being. Vessels were ordered and a service was organised from the town to Glasgow with calls at ports in the east side of Kintyre and the west side of Arran. This was soon buildt up into a successful business which carried both passengers and cargo and saw off any attempts at competition.

This happy state of affairs continued up until the beginning of the 20thth century when a formidable competitor emerged in the form of Williamson's Turbine Steamers which very quickly creamed off a large proportion of the summer passenger traffic while ignoring the cargo traffic. This had an effect on the Campbeltown Company which saw its profits taking a dip. However, a goodly number of passengers stayed loyal to the old company, principally because they were cheaper to use although passage times by necessity had to be longer. With a fleet of two vessels a daily service was maintained except on Sundays and they continued to prosper.

This continued on to the 1930's when the tide very decidedly turned against them. They continued to face the competition of the turbine steamers but now also faced competition from the motor coach. Road transport also began to make inroads into the carriage of cargo. Thus by the 1930's, the Company was seriously considering its future.

Clyde Cargo Steamers

Prior to the Great War a web of cargo services was operated on the Clyde by a variety of companies. Thus, Hill and Company served the towns on the Upper Firth, John Williamson served, Dunoon, Rothesay and the Kyles of Bute piers and MacBrayne and the Minard Castle Shipping Company served the Kyles piers and Loch Fyne. By 1915 the Admiralty wanted to cut the provision of services to the bare bone to save both money and coal and requested that the companies come together into one organization. This they did and Clyde Cargo Steamers were formed. Services were reorganised and united in a very successful manner, so much so that after the war was over the constituents decided to keep Clyde Cargo Steamers going.

They organised services so that vessels left Glasgow every weekday at ungodly hours in the morning to reach all parts of the Foirth while a thrice weekly service ran from Inveraray and other Loch Fyne ports to Glasgow. All sorts of goods were carried and the vessels invariably left the city with cargo piled up everywhere, becoming a ubiquitous site on the Firth in the process.

As well as operating their own services Clyde Cargo Steamers also had some shares in the Campbeltown Company and in the 1930's MacBrayne was interested in acquiring these. This developed into the situation that both companies amalgamated in 1937 under the ownership of MacBrayne. Thus, a new company was born, the Clyde and Campbeltown Shipping Company to operate all the services and funnels were repainted in MacBrayne colours of red with black top. By the beginning of the Second War the company had decided to cease the passenger service to Campbeltown and replace it with a cargo only one.

APPENDIX 3 - FLEET LIST

Name	Built	Builder	Owner (When Picture Taken)	Propulsion	Length (ft)	Gross Tons	Disposed
Arran	1926	Ayrshire Dockyard, Irvine	Clyde Cargo Steamers	Steam Single Screw	99	132	1932
Arran	1933	Ardrossan Dockyard	Clyde Cargo Steamers (see Note)	Steam Single Screw	120	208	1958
Atalanta	1906	J Brown, Clydebank	LM&SR	Turbine Triple Screws Direct Drive	210	486	1937
Ardyne	1928	Scott & Sons, Bowling	Clyde Cargo Steamers (see Note)	Steam Single Screw	135	242	1955
B L Nairn	1929	Caledon Shipbuilding, Dundee	Dundee Harbour Trustees	Paddle Compound Diagonal Disconnecting	162	395	1966
Bute 4	1898	J Fullerton, Paisley	Clyde Cargo Steamers (see Note)	Steam Single Screw	115	174	1935
Caledonia	1889	J Reid, Port Glasgow	LM&SR (CSP)	Paddle Compound Diagonal One Crank	200	244	1933
Caledonia	1934	Wm Denny, Dumbarton	LM&SR (CSP)	Paddle Triple Expansion Diagonal	223	624	1970
Columba	1878	J & G Thomson, Clydebank	David MacBrayne	Paddle Two Cylinder Oscillating	301	602	1936
Comet	1905	A W Robertson, London	David MacBrayne	Paraffin Twin Screw	65	43	1947
Dalriada	1926	R Duncan, Port Glasgow	Campbeltown & Glasgow (see Note)	Steam Single Screw	230	758	1942
Davaar	1885	London & Glasgow, Govan	Campbeltown & Glasgow (see Note)	Steam Single Screw	217	535	1943
Duchess of Argyll	1906	Wm Denny, Dumbarton	LM&SR (CSP)	Turbine Triple Screws Direct Drive	250	593	1952
Duchess of Fife	1903	Fairfield, Govan	LM&SR (CSP)	Paddle Four Cylinders Diagonal Two Cranks	210	336	1953
Duchess of Hamilton	1932	Harland & Wolff, Govan	LM&SR (CSP)	Turbine Triple Screws Direct Drive	262	795	1970
Duchess of Montrose	1930	Wm Denny, Dumbarton	LM&SR (CSP)	Turbine Triple Screws Direct Drive	262	806	1965
Duchess of Rothesay	1895	J & G Thomson, Clydebank	LM&SR (CSP)	Paddle Compound Diagonal Two Cranks	225	338	1946
Eagle III	1910	Napier & Miller, Old Kilpatrick	Williamson-Buchanan	Paddle Single Diagonal	215	432	1946
Empress	1888	Napier, Shanks & Miller, Yoker	LM&SR & L&NER	Paddle Single Diagonal Two Cylinder	165	229	1933
Fair Maid	1886	S McKnight & Co, Ayr	Grangemouth & Forth Towing	Paddle Compound Diagonal One Crank	190	211	1945
Fusilier	1888	McArthur & Co, Paisley	David MacBrayne	Paddle Single Diagonal Two Cylinder	202	280	1934
Glencoe	1846	Tod & McGregor, Govan	David MacBrayne	Paddle Single Steeple	165	226	1931
Glen Rosa	1893	J & G Thomson, Clydebank	LM&SR	Paddle Compound Diagonal Two Cranks	200	306	1939
Glen Sannox	1925	Wm Denny, Dumbarton	LM&SR	Turbine Triple Screws Direct Drive	249	664	1954
Gondolier	1866	J & G Thomson, Govan	David MacBrayne	Paddle Two Cylinder Oscillating	148	173	1940
Iona	1864	J & G Thomson, Govan	David MacBrayne	Paddle Two Cylinder Oscillating	255	396	1936
Isle of Arran	1892	T B Seath, Rutherglen	Williamson-Buchanan	Paddle Single Diagonal	210	313	1933
Jeanie Deans	1931	Fairfield, Govan	L&NER	Paddle Triple Expansion Diagonal	250	635	1965
Juno	1898	Clydebank Engineering	LM&SR	Paddle Compound Diagonal Two Cranks	245	592	1932
Juno	1937	Fairfield, Govan	LM&SR (CSP)	Paddle Triple Expansion Diagonal	223	642	1941
Jupiter	1896	J & G Thomson, Clydebank	LM&SR	Paddle Compound Diagonal Two Cranks	230	394	1935
Jupiter	1937	Fairfield, Govan	LM&SR (CSP)	Paddle Triple Expansion Diagonal	223	642	1961
Kenilworth	1898	A & J Inglis, Pointhouse	L&NER	Paddle Single Diagonal	215	390	1938
King Edward	1901	Wm Denny, Dumbarton	Williamson-Buchanan	Turbine Triple Screws Direct Drive	250	551	1952
King George V	1926	Wm Denny, Dumbarton	Turbine Steamers (Williamson) to 1935 / David MacBrayne from 1936	Turbine Twin Screws Geared Drive	260	789	1974
Kylemore	1897	Russell & Co, Port Glasgow	Williamson-Buchanan	Paddle Compound Diagonal Two Cranks	200	319	1940
Lady Clare	1891	J McArthur, Paisley	Moville Steamship Co	Paddle Single Diagonal	180	257	1928
Lochbroom	1871	J Elder, Govan	David MacBrayne	Steam Single Screw	241	1139	1937
Lochearn	1930	Ardrossan Dockyard	David MacBrayne	Diesel Twin Screw	155	542	1964
Lochfyne	1931	Wm Denny, Dumbarton	David MacBrayne	Diesel Electric Twin Screw	209	748	1970
Lochiel	1906	Scott of Kinghorn	David MacBrayne	Steam Single Screw	140	318	1938
Lochmor	1930	Ardrossan Dockyard	David MacBrayne	Diesel Twin Screw	155	542	1964
Lochness	1929	Harland & Wolff, Govan	David MacBrayne	Steam Twin Screw	200	777	1955
Lochnevis	1934	Wm Denny, Dumbarton	David MacBrayne	Diesel Electric Twin Screw	175	568	1970
Lord of the Isles	1891	D & W Henderson, Partick	Turbine Steamers (Williamson)	Paddle Two Cylinder Oscillating	255	466	1928
Lucy Ashton	1888	T B Seath, Rutherglen	L&NER	Paddle Compound Diagonal Two Cranks	190	224	1949
Marchioness of Breadalbane	1890	J Reid, Port Glasgow	LM&SR (CSP)	Paddle Compound Diagonal One Crank	200	246	1935
Marchioness of Graham	1936	Fairfield, Govan	LM&SR (CSP)	Turbine Twin Screws Geared Drive	220	585	1958
Marchioness of Lorne	1935	Fairfield, Govan	LM&SR (CSP)	Paddle Triple Expansion Diagonal	199	449	1955
Marmion	1906	A & J Inglis, Pointhouse	L&NER	Paddle Compound Diagonal Two Cranks	210	409	1941
Mercury	1892	Napier, Shanks & Bell, Yoker	LM&SR	Paddle Compound Diagonal Two Cranks	220	378	1933
Mercury	1934	Fairfield, Govan	LM&SR	Paddle Triple Expansion Diagonal	223	621	1940
Minard	1926	Scott & Sons, Bowling	Clyde Cargo Steamers (see Note)	Steam Single Screw	143	241	1955
Mountaineer	1910	A & J Inglis, Pointhouse	David MacBrayne	Paddle Compound Diagonal Two Cranks	180	235	1938
Pioneer	1905	A & J Inglis, Pointhouse	David MacBrayne	Paddle Compound Diagonal Two Cranks	160	241	1944
Plover	1904	Scott & Sons, Bowling	David MacBrayne	Steam Single Screw	136	229	1946
Prince Edward	1911	A & J Inglis, Pointhouse	LM&SR & L&NER	Paddle Compound Diagonal Two Cranks	175	304	1955
Prince George	1898	A & J Inglis, Pointhouse	LM&SR & L&NER	Paddle Single Diagonal Two Cylinder	165	256	1942
Princess Louise	1898	Ritchie, Graham & Milne, Govan	David MacBrayne	Steam Single Screw	95	106	1939
Princess May	1898	A & J Inglis, Pointhouse	LM&SR & L&NER	Paddle Single Diagonal Two Cylinder	165	256	1953
Princess Patricia	1905	J & I Thornycroft, Southampton	LM&SR & L&NER	Paddle Compound Diagonal Two Cranks	130	127	1939
Queen Alexandra to 1935 / Saint Columba from 1936	1912	Wm Denny, Dumbarton	Turbine Steamers (Williamson) to 1935 / David MacBrayne from 1936	Turbine Triple Screws Direct Drive	270	785 / 827	1958
Queen-Empress	1912	Murdoch & Murray, Port Glasgow	Williamson-Buchanan	Paddle Compound Diagonal Two Cranks	210	411	1946
Queen Mary	1933	Wm Denny, Dumbarton	Williamson-Buchanan	Turbine Triple Screws Direct Drive	252	870	1977
Talisman	1896	A & J Inglis, Pointhouse	L&NER	Paddle Single Diagonal	215	293	1934
Talisman	1935	A & J Inglis, Pointhouse	L&NER	Paddle Diesel Electric	215	450	1967
Waverley	1899	A & J Inglis, Pointhouse	L&NER	Paddle Compound Diagonal Two Cranks	235	537	1940
Wee Cumbrae	1935	Wm Denny, Dumbarton	LM&SR (CSP)	Diesel Twin Screw	59	37	1953
William Muir	1879	John Key, Kirkcaldy	L&NER	Paddle Compound Diagonal Two Cranks	174	364	1937

Note: Clyde Cargo Steamers and Campbeltown & Glasgow Steam Packet Joint Stock Company combined in 1937 to form Clyde & Campbeltown Shipping Company

ABOUT THE PADDLE STEAMER PRESERVATION SOCIETY

About the PSPS

The Paddle Steamer Preservation Society (PSPS) is Britain's largest and most successful steamship preservation group with around 2500 members. Since its formation in 1959, the PSPS has saved two historic paddle steamers – PS Waverley and PS Kingswear Castle – both in service in the UK.

The PSPS has provided over £3.8 million to ensure Waverley continues to sail, making the Society the single largest Waverley supporter group. The PSPS has also provided over £600,000 to enable works on Kingswear Castle to ensure her future. As a charity, the PSPS welcomes bequests and legacies. We invite you to join us and play your part to help keep both ships sailing.

Benefits of PSPS Membership

- Support for Waverley & Kingswear Castle
- 2 Free Waverley tickets for children each year
- Free full colour A4 "Paddle Wheels" magazine every 3 months
- Access discounted Waverley Cruising Vouchers
- Regular meetings across the UK
- Enjoy your next Waverley cruise at half price when you join PSPS aboard Waverley

Full details of all membership benefits from our website at paddlesteamers.org/join

The Paddle Steamer Preservation Society is a Company limited by Guarantee No. 2167853 (England & Wales). It is a Charity registered in England & Wales (298328) and in Scotland (SC037603). Registered Office: Mayfield, Hoe Lane, Abinger Hammer, Dorking RH5 6RS.

Aims of the PSPS

- To preserve Paddle Steamers in operation in the UK

- To communicate the historic significance of Paddle Steamers in the Nation's maritime and industrial heritage

- To acquire, preserve and exhibit a collection of equipment and material associated with Paddle Steamers

The PSPS Collection

The PSPS Collection continues to expand with over 50,000 items. This is the largest collection of materials relating to Paddle Steamers including postcards, sailing bills, books, souvenirs and fittings from much loved steamers of the past. We welcome further donations to enhance our collection.

Paddle Wheels

Each issue of the magazine gives the latest news on Waverley and Kingswear Castle, as well as regular updates on Maid of the Loch and Medway Queen. Also included are articles on steamers of the past, items in our collection, and local Branch meetings.

Social Media Channels

With regular updates on the Society and our ships

- paddlesteamers
- @PSPS_UK
- PSPS Scottish Branch
- psps_uk

Contact PSPS

membership@paddlesteamers.org

38 Merrylee Park Avenue, Giffnock, Glasgow G46 6HR